EASY PIANO

American Idol

Sheet Music Hits
Favorite Songs from Seasons 1–4

Arranged by Dan Coates

Contents

Title	American Idol Performer	Page
8th World Wonder	Kimberly Locke	50
All-American Girl	Carrie Underwood	2
Amazed	Joshua Gracin	10
As Time Goes By	John Stevens	7
At Last	Christina Christian	14
Breakaway	Kelly Clarkson	17
Bridge over Troubled Water	Clay Aiken	22
Celebrate Me Home	Ruben Studdard	29
Circle of Life, The	Jennifer Hudson	34
Dance with My Father	Scott Savol	36
Desperado	Camile Velasco	40
Don't Rain on My Parade	La Toya London	44
If Ever I Would Leave You	Anwar Robinson	54
Inside Your Heaven	Carrie Underwood	58
Moon River	Anwar Robinson	26
Music of My Heart	Ruben Studdard	62
(I Can't Get No) Satisfaction	Bo Bice	66
Summertime	Fantasia Barrino	70
Weekend in New England	Jennifer Hudson	76
When a Man Loves a Woman	Christina Christian	80
When You Tell Me That You Love Me	Season 4 finalists	84
A Whole New World	Ruben Studdard	73

American Idol™ 19 TV Ltd & FremantleMedia North America, Inc.
Licensed by FremantleMedia Enterprises.
www.americanidol.com

Copyright © MMIX by Alfred Publishing Co., Inc.
All rights reserved.   Printed in USA.
ISBN-10: 0-7390-5777-4
ISBN-13: 978-0-7390-5777-3

ALL-AMERICAN GIRL

Words and Music by Carrie Underwood,
Kellie Lovelace and Ashley Gorley
Arranged by Dan Coates

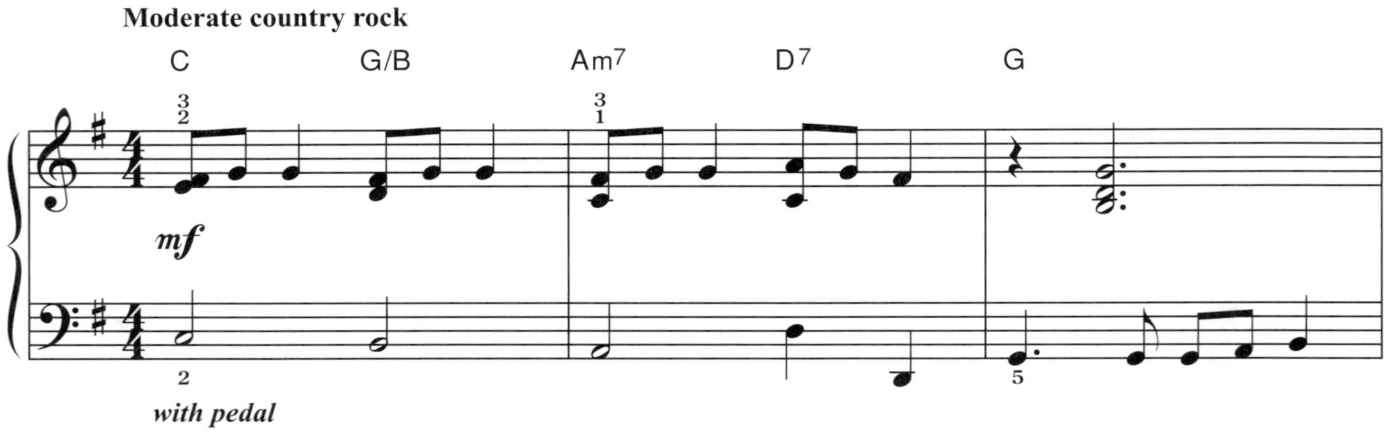

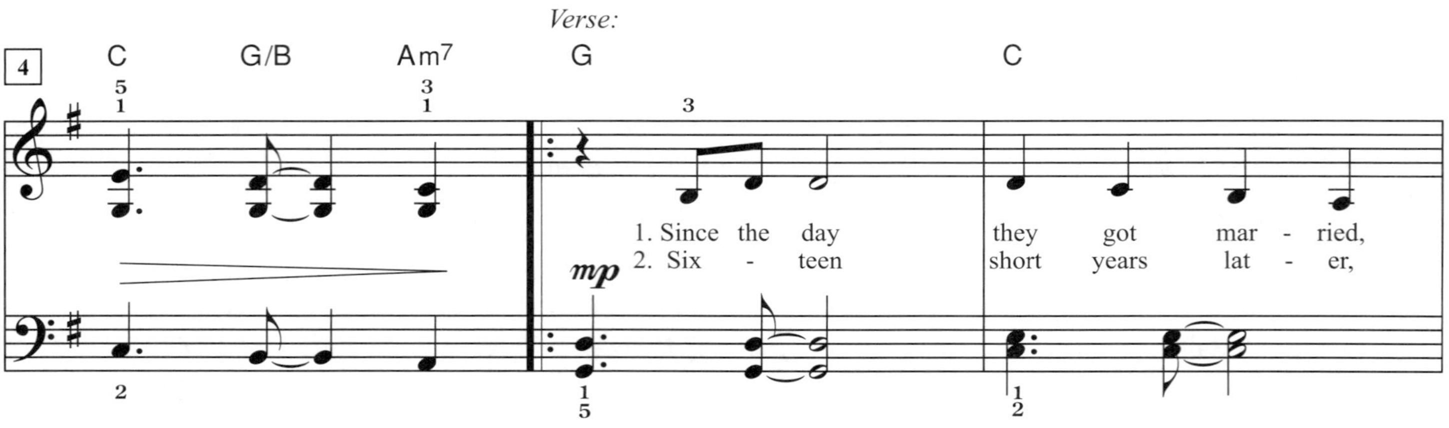

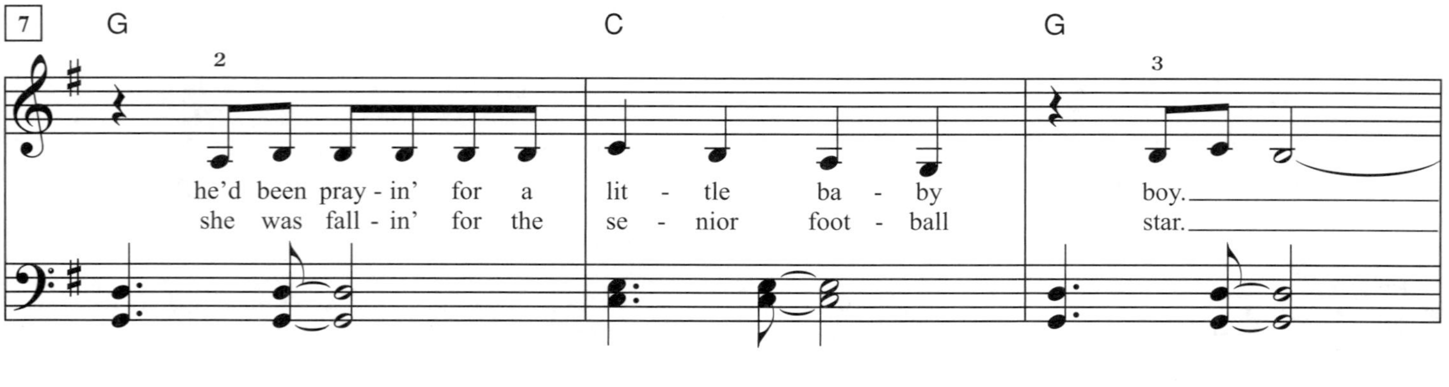

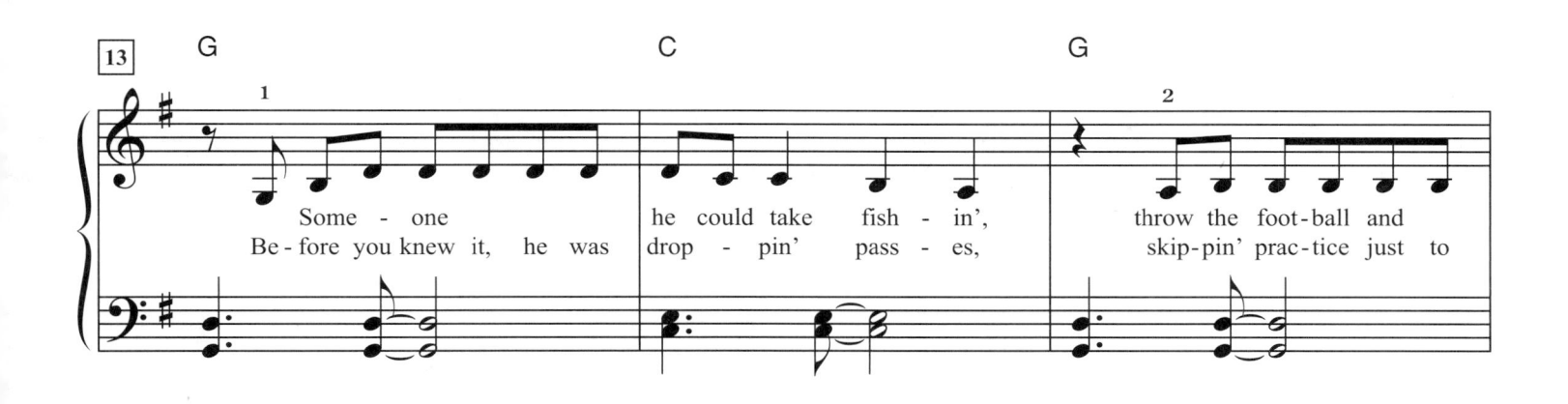

Some - one he could take fish - in', throw the foot - ball and
Be - fore you knew it, he was drop - pin' pass - es, skip - pin' prac - tice just to

be his pride and joy.
spend more time with her.

He could al - read - y see him
The coach said, "Hey, son,

22
C D G/B C
hold - in' that tro - phy, tak - in' his team to state. But when the
what's your prob - lem? Tell me, have you lost your mind?"
25
D G/B C G/B Am7
nurse came in with a lit - tle pink blan - ket, all those big dreams
Dad - dy said, "You'll lose your free ride to col - lege. Boy, you'd bet - ter tell her good -
28
Chorus:
D C G
changed. And now he's wrapped a - round her fin - ger. She's the
bye." But,
mf
31
D Em C
cen - ter of his whole world. And his heart be - longs

to that sweet little, beau-ti-ful, won-der-ful, per-fect All-A-mer-i-can...

girl.

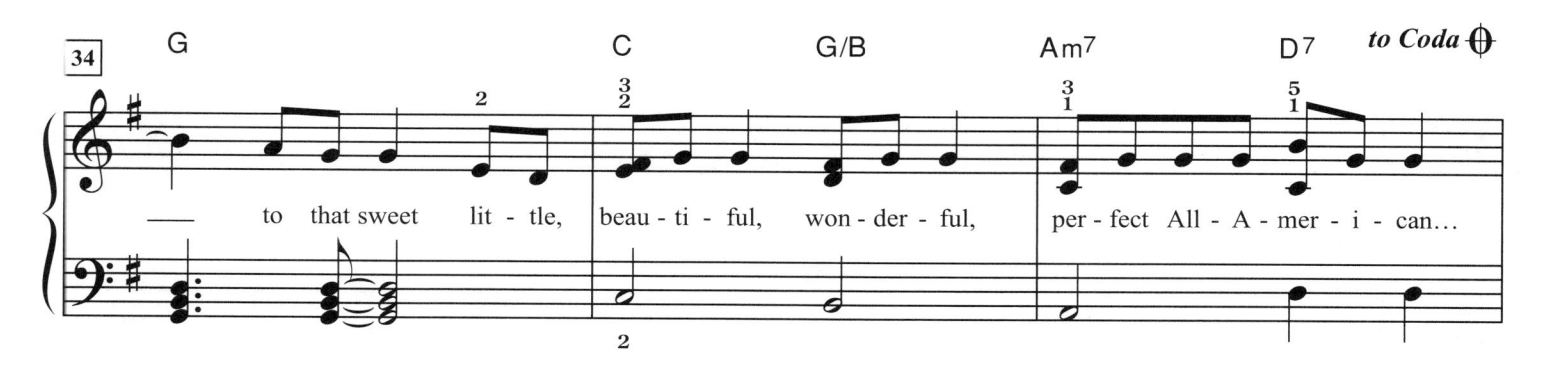

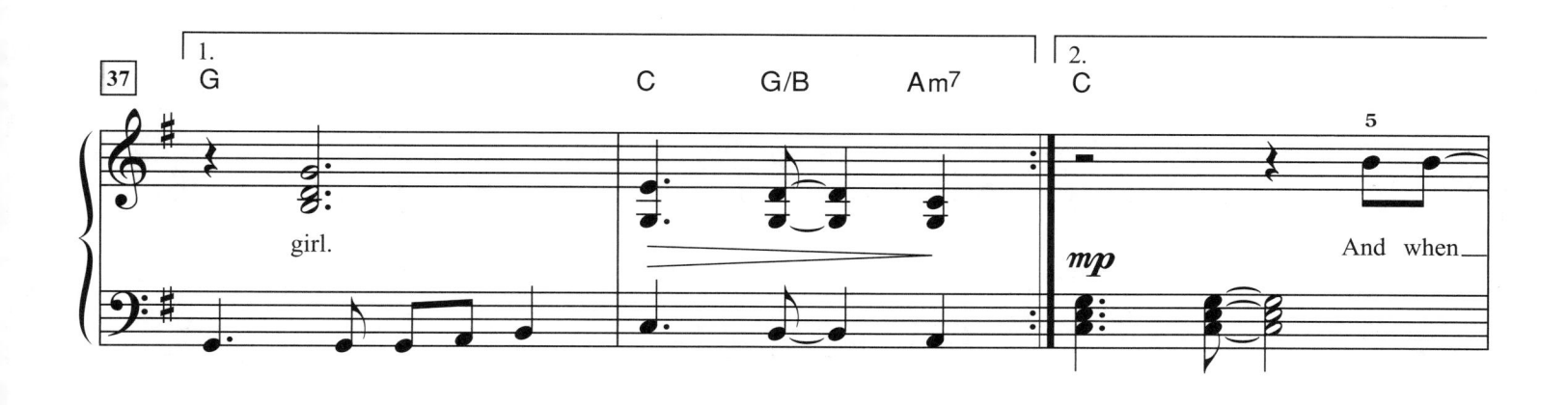

And when they got mar-ried and de-cid-ed to have one of their own,

she said, "Be hon-est, tell me what you want." And he said, "Hon-ey, you ought-a know,

46
C G/B Am7 G/B
a sweet lit - tle, beau - ti - ful, oh, a
49
C G/B Am7 D7
D.S. al Coda
beau - ti - ful, won - der - ful, per - fect All - A - mer - i - can...
cresc.
Coda
G C G/B Am7
girl.
53
G C G/B Am7 G
mp
molto rit.

AS TIME GOES BY

Words and Music by Herman Hupfeld
Arranged by Dan Coates

10
A7 Dm7 G7 Gm/D G7
And when two lov - ers woo, they still say, "I love you," on
mp
13
C Dm7 D♯dim7 C/E Am7 D7 Dm7 G7
that you can re - ly; no mat - ter what the fu - ture brings, as time goes
17
C F Fm C/E C7 F
by. Moon - light and love songs
mf
20
A7 Dm D♯dim
nev - er out of date, hearts full of pas - sion, jeal - ou - sy and hate;

23
Am/E F7 D7 G7 C♯dim7
wom - an needs man and man must have his mate; that no one can de -
f
26
Dm7 G7 Dm7 G7 Gm/D G7
ny. It's still the same old sto - ry, a fight for love and glo - ry, a
mp
29
C Dm7 D♯dim7 C/E Am7 D7
case of do or die! The world will al - ways wel - come
mf
32
C/E A7 Dm7 G
1. C A7
2. C
lov - ers, as time goes by. You by.
mp
p

AMAZED

Words and Music by
Marv Green, Aimee Mayo, and Chris Lindsey
Arranged by Dan Coates

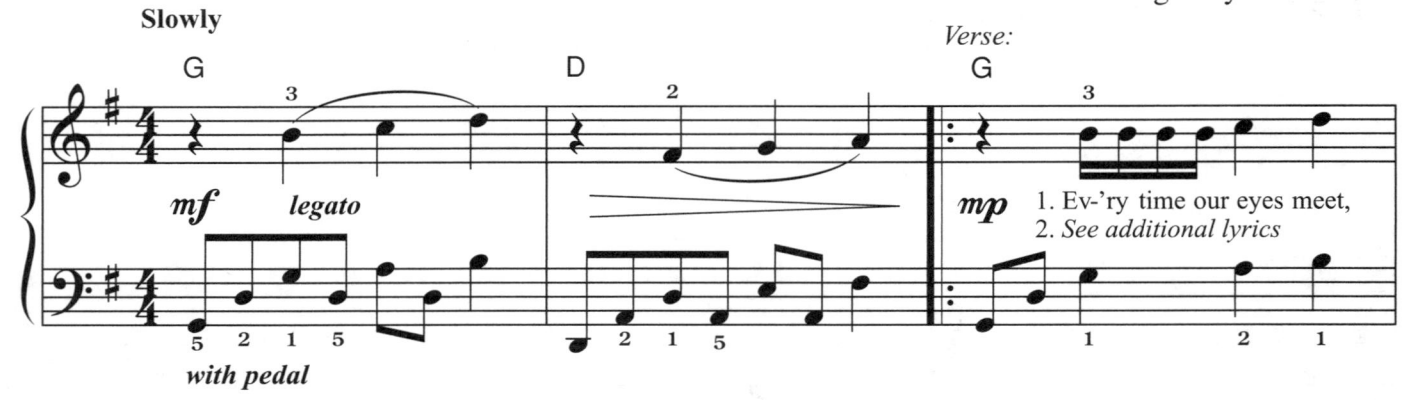

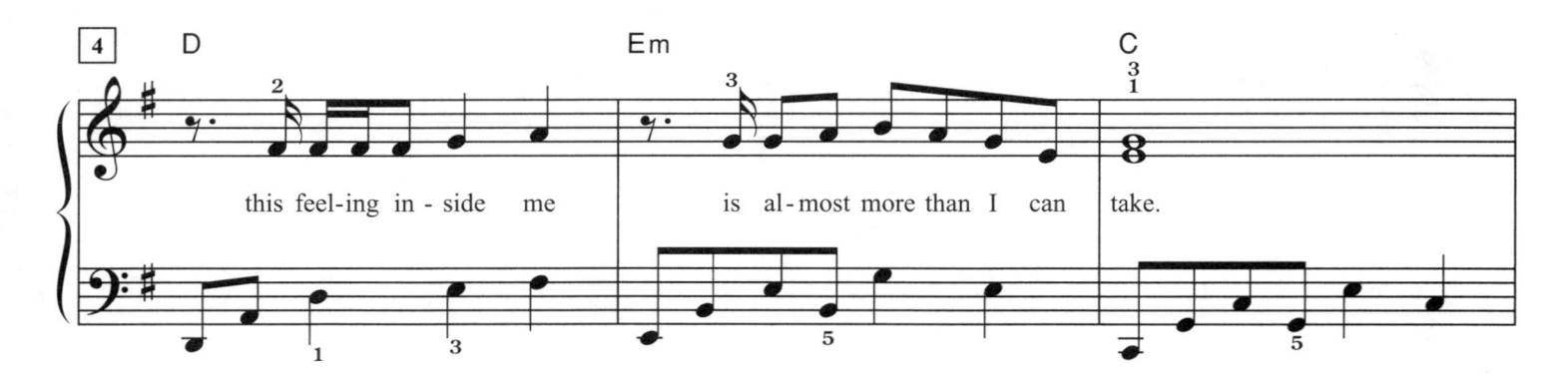

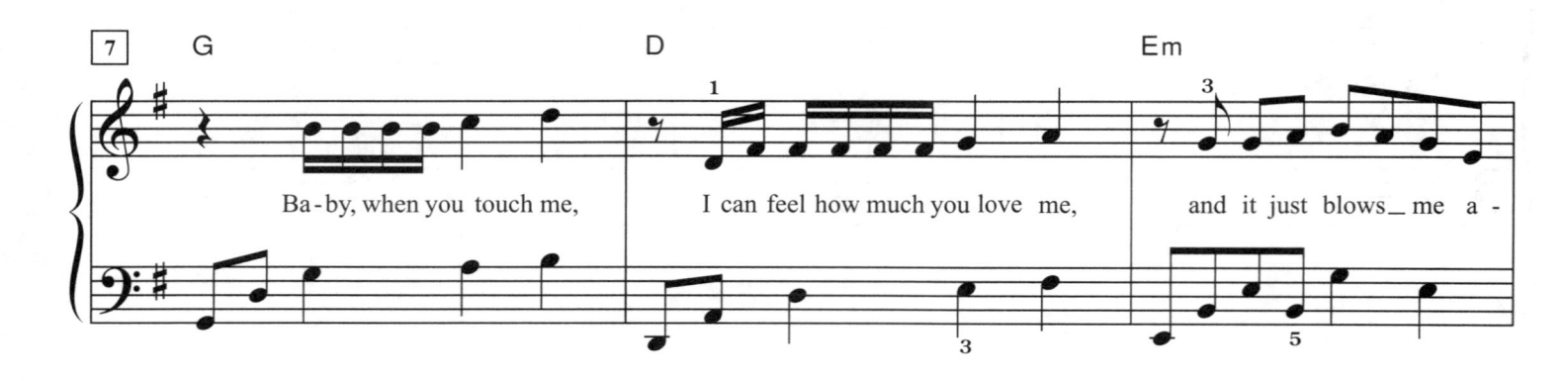

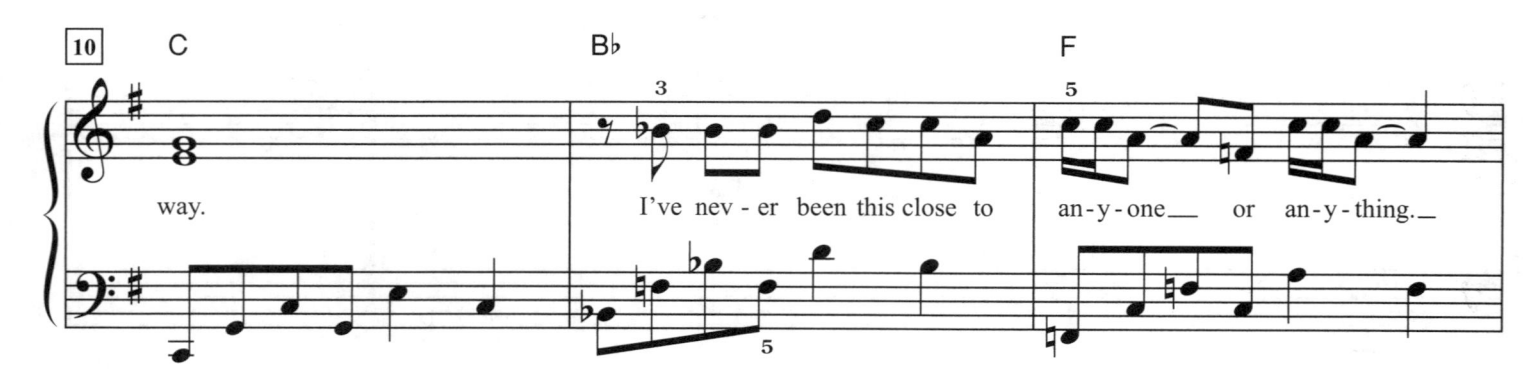

Lyrics:

1. Ev'ry time our eyes meet, this feeling inside me is almost more than I can take. Baby, when you touch me, I can feel how much you love me, and it just blows me away. I've never been this close to anyone or anything.

© 1999 WARNER-TAMERLANE PUBLISHING CORP., GOLDEN WHEAT MUSIC,
CAREERS-BMG PUBLISHING, INC. and SONGS OF DREAMWORKS (Admin. by CHERRY RIVER MUSIC CO.)
All Rights for GOLDEN WHEAT MUSIC Administered by WARNER-TAMERLANE PUBLISHING CORP.
All Rights Reserved

13
Gm
Eb
I can hear your thoughts,
I can see your dreams.
Chorus:
15
C
G
Am
mf
I don't know how you do what you do.
I'm so in love with
you.
It just keeps get-ting bet -
18
F
C
G
ter.
I wan-na spend the rest of my life
with you by my side
21
Am
G
F
Eb
for-ev - er and ev - er.
Ev-'ry lit-tle thing that you

24 F
1. G D
do, ba-by, I'm a-mazed by you.
dim.
2. 27 G Bb C G
you.
mf
30 Bb F C G
f
Ev-'ry lit-tle thing that you do, I'm so in love with
33 Am F C
you. It just keeps get-ting bet - ter.
I wan-na spend the rest of my life

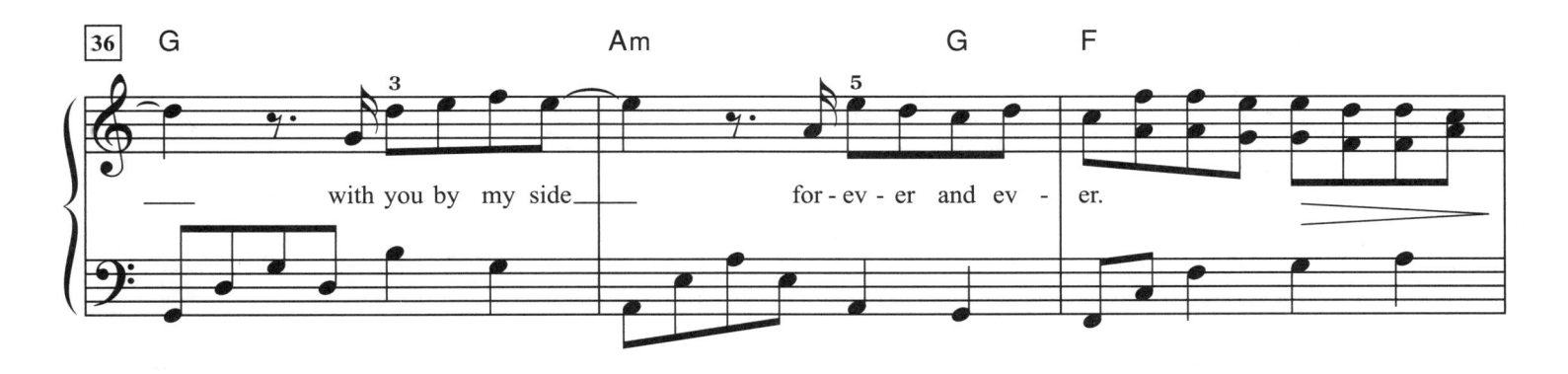

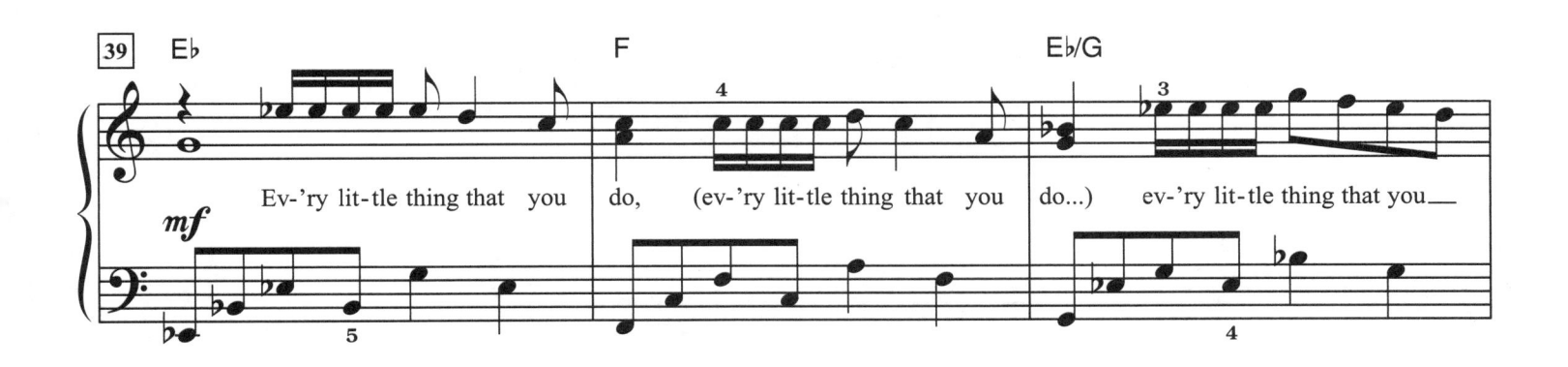

Verse 2:
The smell of your skin,
The taste of your kiss,
The way you whisper in the dark.
Your hair all around me,
Baby, you surround me.
You touch every place in my heart.
Oh, it feels like the first time every time.
I wanna spend the whole night in your eyes.
(To Chorus:)

AT LAST

Music by Harry Warren
Lyric by Mack Gordon
Arranged by Dan Coates

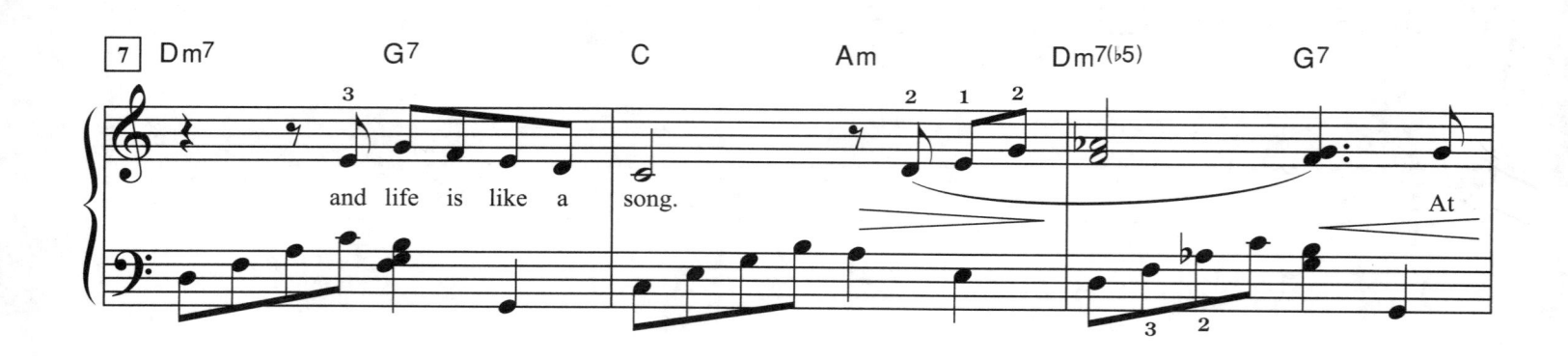

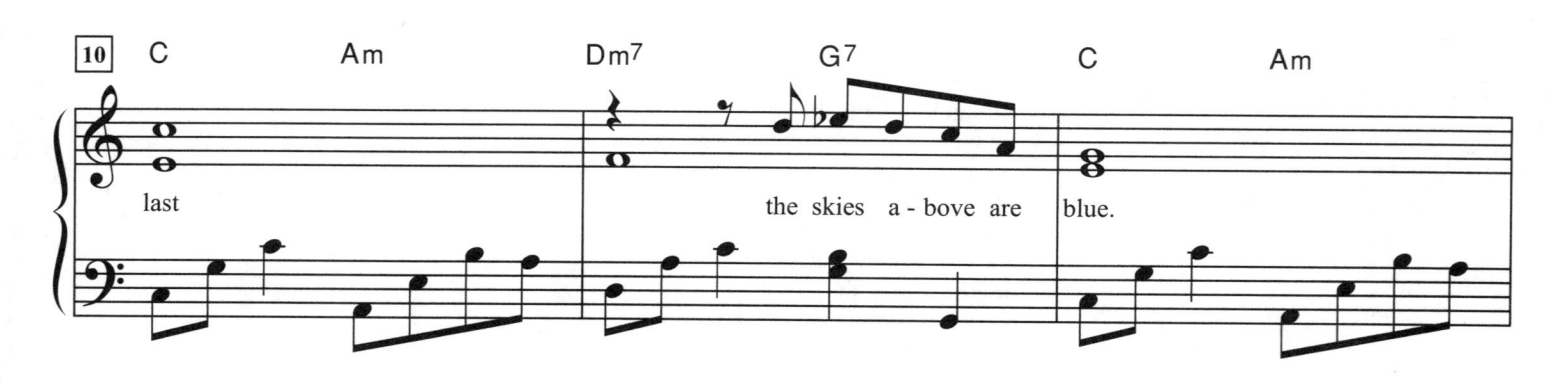

13 Dm7 G7 C Am Dm7 G7
My heart was wrapped in clo - ver the night I looked at
16 C Fm G7 C F G7
you. I found a dream that I can
mp
19 F/C C F♯m7(♭5) B7 Em
speak to, a dream that I can call my own. I found a
22 Cm/E♭ D7 G Am7 D7
thrill to press my cheek to, a thrill I've nev - er
mf

25
G7sus G7 C Am Dm7 G7
known. You smiled and then the spell was
f
28
C(add 9) Am Dm7 G7 C Am
cast. And here we are in heav - en
31
1.
Dm7 G7 C Am Dm7(♭5) G7
for you are mine at last. At
mf
34
2.
Dm7 G7 C Fm C
for you are mine at last.
rit.
mf

BREAKAWAY

*Words and Music by Matthew Gerrard,
Bridget Benenate and Avril Lavigne
Arranged by Dan Coates*

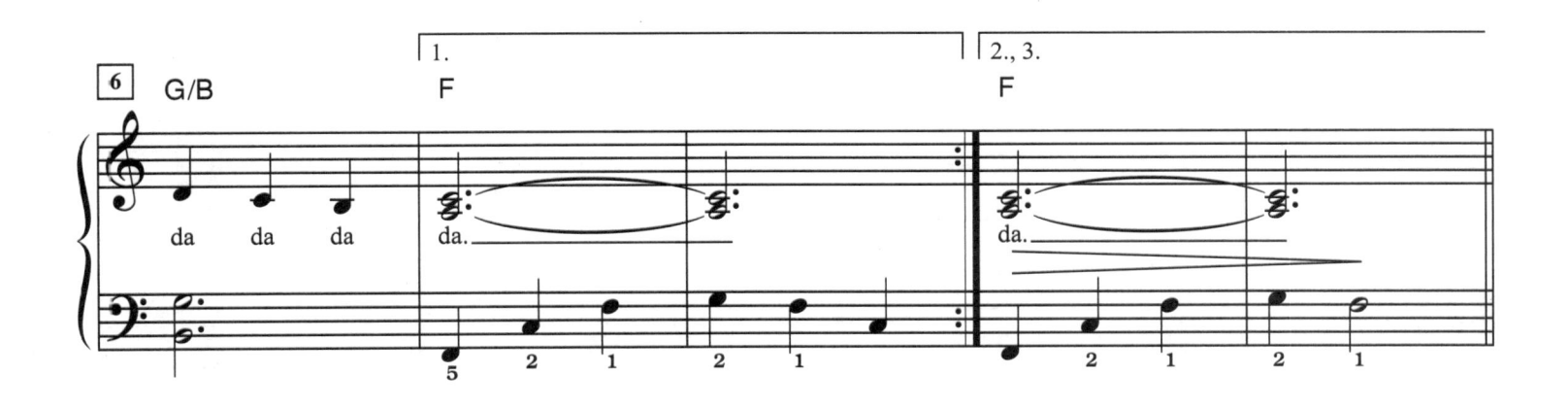

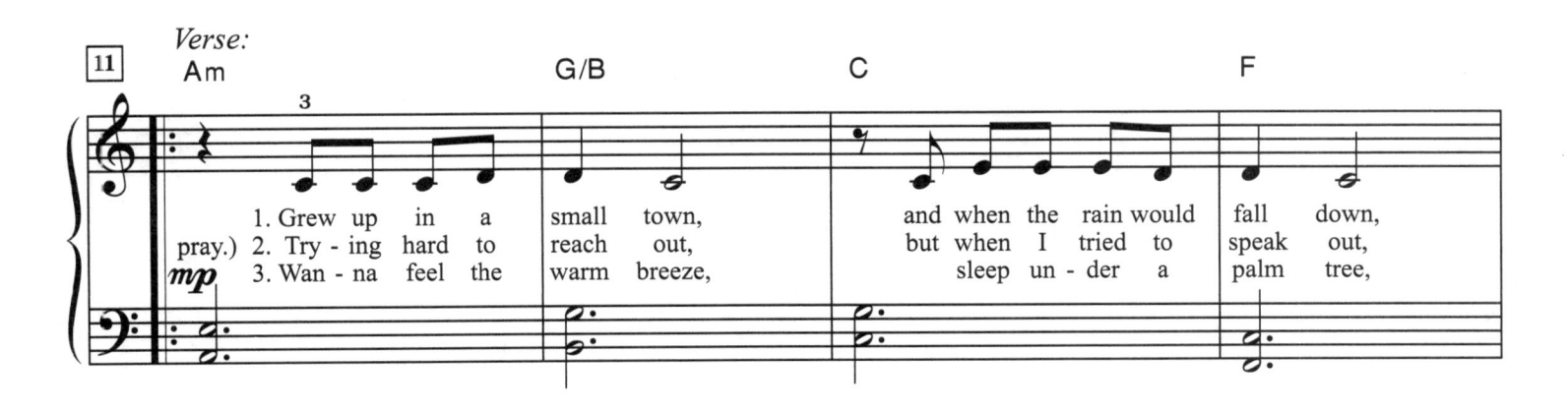

© 2004 WB MUSIC CORP., G MATT MUSIC, WINDSWEPT MUSIC and ALMO MUSIC CORPORATION
All Rights on behalf of Itself and G MATT MUSIC Administered by WB MUSIC CORP.
All Rights Reserved

15
Am G/B F
I'd just stare out my win - dow,
felt like no one could hear me.
feel the rush of the o - cean.
19
Am G/B C F
dream-in' of what could be, and if I'd end up hap - py.
Want - ed to be - long here, but some-thing felt so wrong here
Get on board a fast train, trav - el on a jet plane,
23
Am G/B F
1.
2., 3.
I would pray. (I would I could
So I pray and
far a - way
28
Am G D F G
cresc.
break - a - way.
break - a - way.

Chorus:
34
C G
mf
I'll spread my wings and I'll learn how to fly, I'll
38
Am F C
do what it takes 'til I touch the sky. And I'll make a wish,
3. Though it's not eas - y to tell you good - bye, got - ta take a risk,
43
C G Am G
take a chance, make a change, and break - a -
48
F C G
way. Out of the dark - ness and in - to the
f

53
Am
F
sun. But I won't for - get {all the ones that I love.} I'll
{the place I come from.}
58
C
G
to Coda
Am
mf
take a risk, take a chance, make a change and break -
63
G
1.
D.C.
2.
F
F
a - way.
way.
Bridge:
68
G
C
F
G
mf
Build - ings with a hun - dred floors, swing - in' 'round re - volv - ing doors. May - be I don't

73
C F G
know where they'll take me, but got - ta keep mov - in' on,
78
D.S. al Coda
C F D F G
mov - in' on. Fly a - way, break - a - way.
Coda
Am G F Am
break - a - way, break -
89
G F Am G F(add 9)
a - way, break - a - way.
mp

BRIDGE OVER TROUBLED WATER

Words and Music by Paul Simon
Arranged by Dan Coates

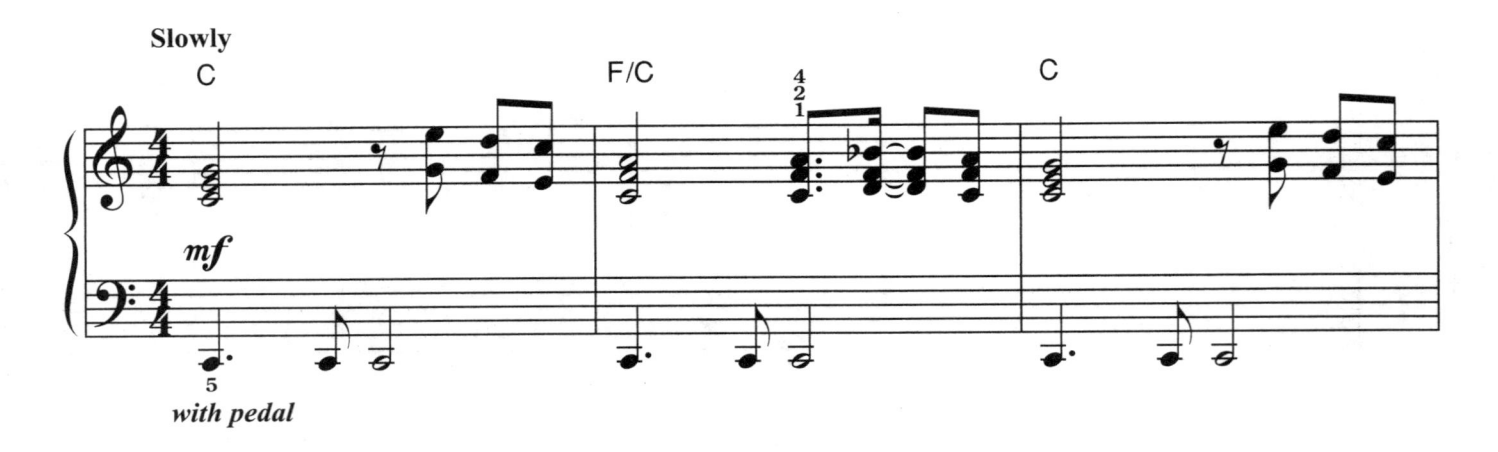

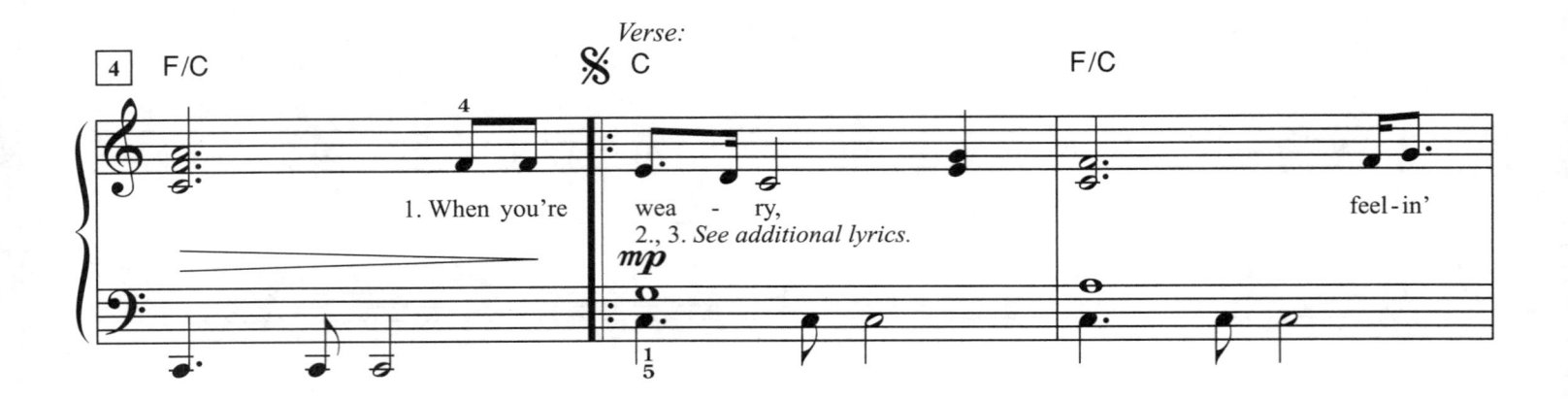

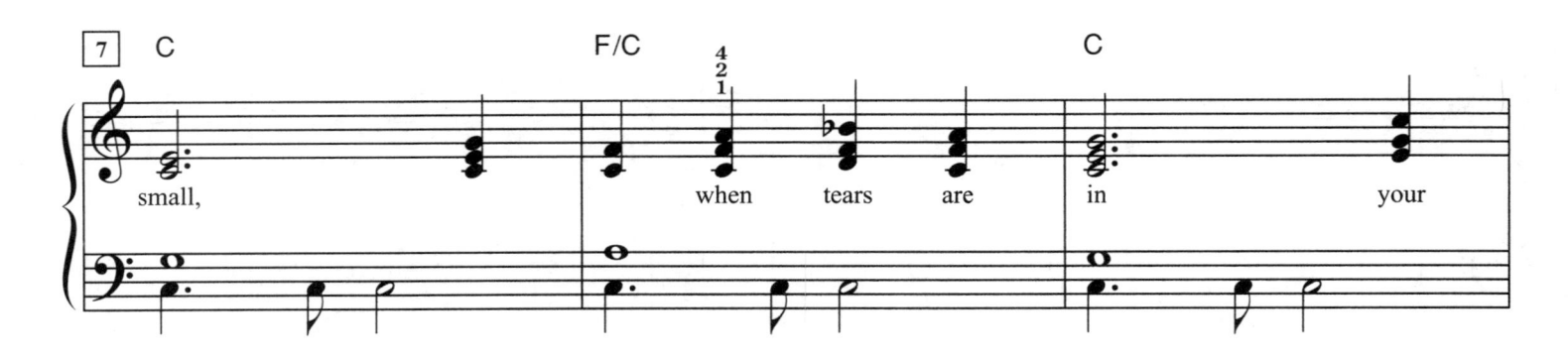

10
F/C C F/C C G/B Am7
eyes, I will dry them all. I'm on your
13
G C Cmaj7
side, oh, when times get rough.
16
C7 F D7 G C C7/E
and friends just can't be found. Like a
cresc.
Chorus:
1.
19
F F♯dim7 C/G Am7 Dm7 Fm C
bridge o - ver trou - bled wa - ter, I will lay me down.
f

23
F/C
C
F/C
2. When you're
Chorus:
2., 3.
26
F
F♯dim7
C/G
Am7
Dm7
E7
bridge o - ver trou - bled wa - ter, I will lay me
f
29
Am
C7
F
F♯dim7
C/G
Am
to Coda
down. Like a bridge o - ver trou - bled wa - ter,
32
Dm7
E7
Am
Am(maj7)
Am7
D7
Fm/A♭
I will lay me down.
ff

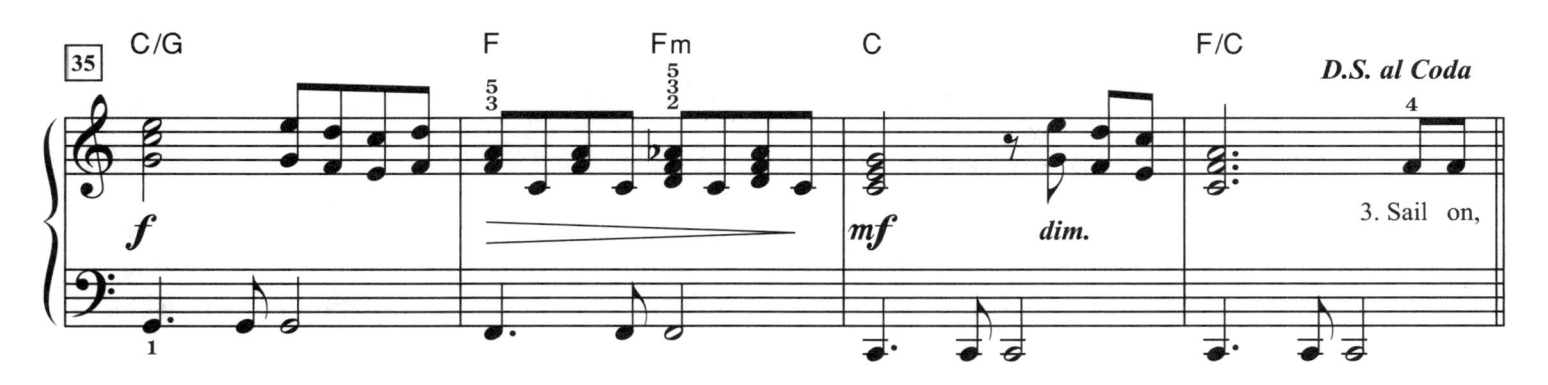

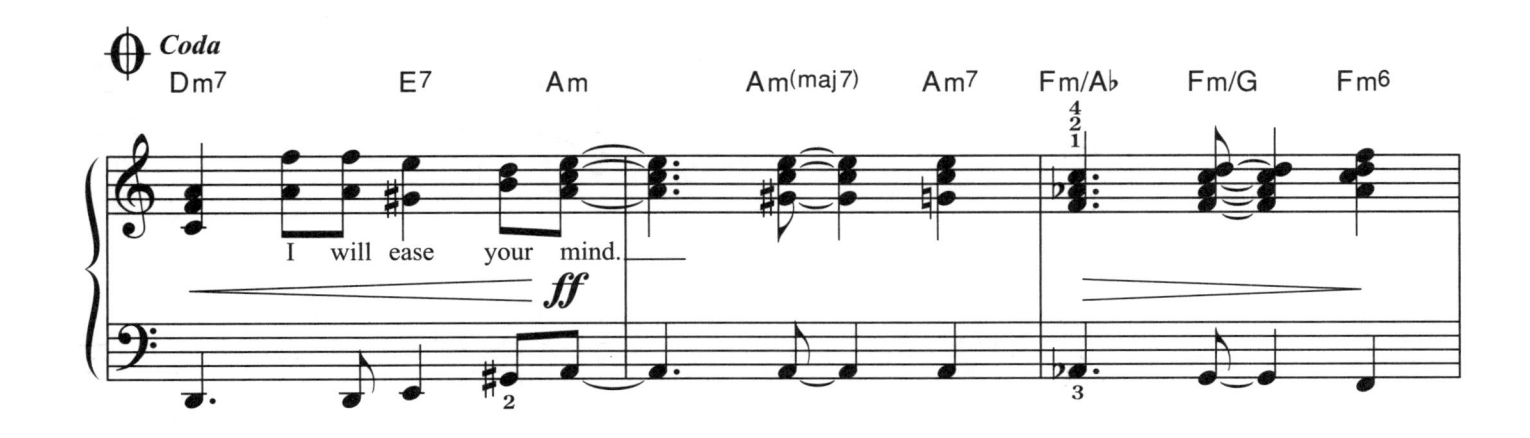

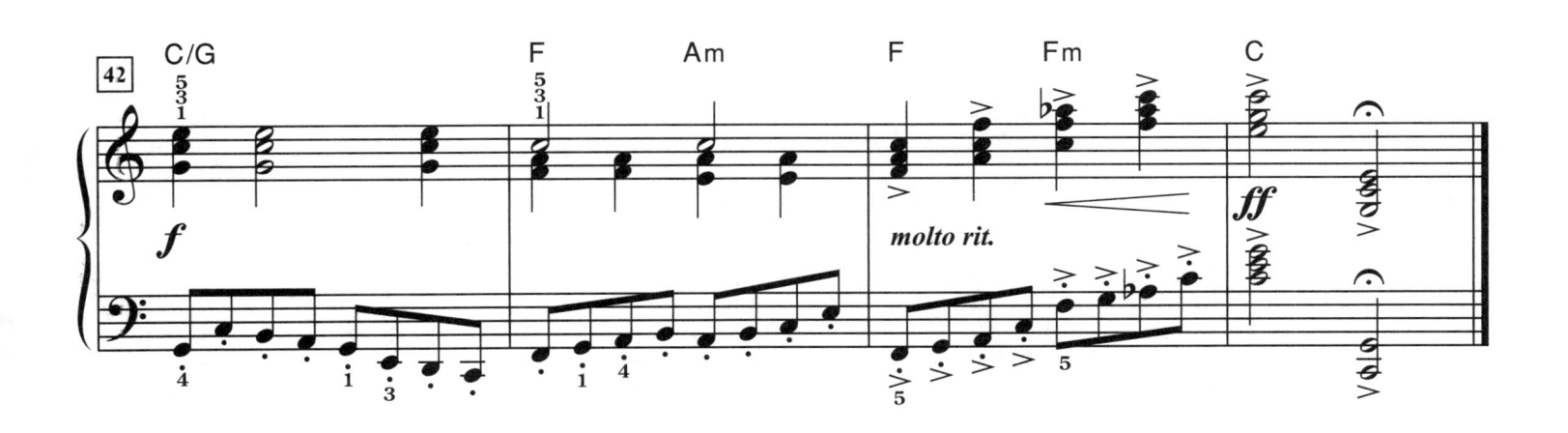

Verse 2:
When you're down and out,
When you're on the street,
When evening falls so hard, I will comfort you.
I'll take your part when darkness comes
And pain is all around.
Like a bridge over troubled water, I will lay me down.
Like a bridge over troubled water, I will lay me down.

Verse 3:
Sail on, silver girl, sail on by.
Your time has come to shine,
All your dreams are on their way.
See how they shine, if you need a friend.
I'm sailing right behind.
Like a bridge over troubled water, I will ease your mind.
Like a bridge over troubled water, I will ease your mind.

MOON RIVER

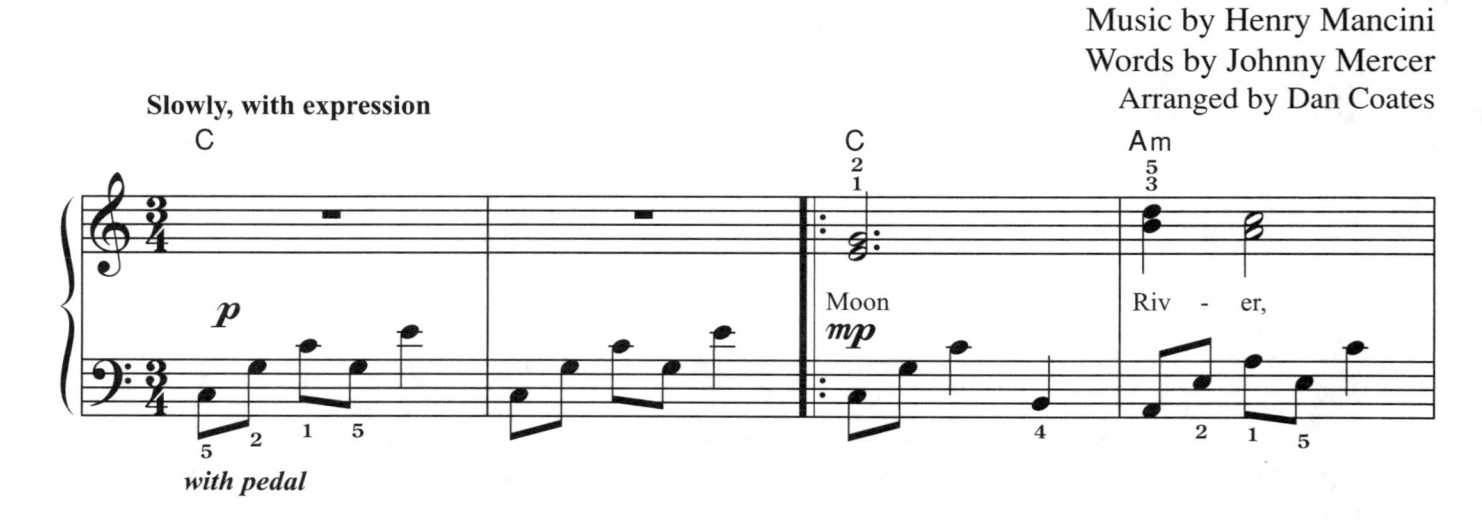

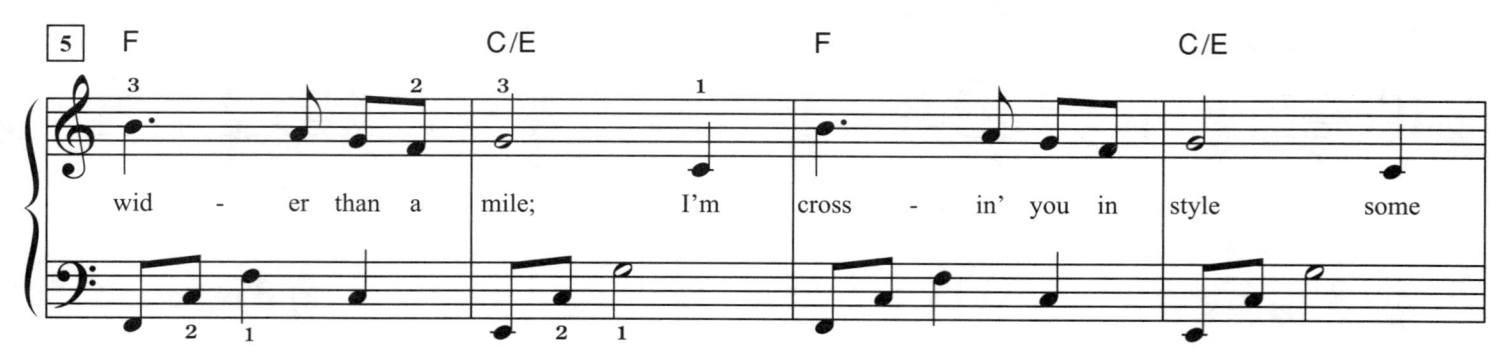

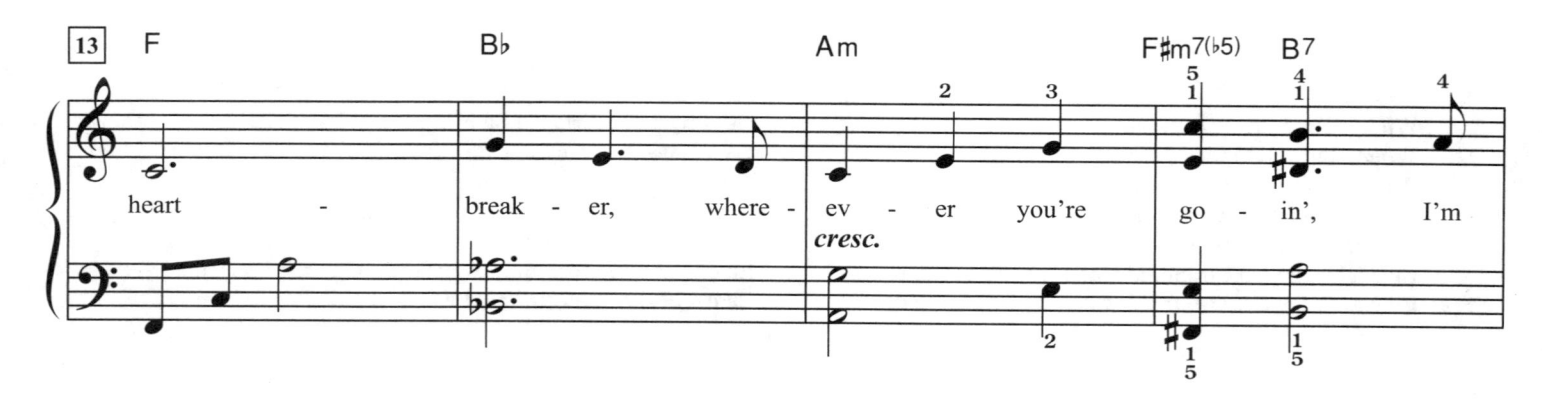

Music by Henry Mancini
Words by Johnny Mercer
Arranged by Dan Coates

Slowly, with expression

with pedal

Moon Riv-er, wid-er than a mile; I'm cross-in' you in style some day. Old dream-mak-er, you heart-break-er, wher-ev-er you're go-in', I'm

© 1961 (Renewed) FAMOUS MUSIC CORPORATION
All Rights Reserved   Used by Permission

17
Em A7 Dm7 G7 C Am
go - in' your way. Two drift - ers,
mf
21
F C/E F C/E
off to see the world, there's such a lot of world to
25
Bm7(♭5) E7sus E7 Am Am7/G
see. We're af - ter the
29
F♯m7(♭5) F7 C/E F
same rain - bow's end, wait - in' 'round the

33
C/E
F
1.
C/E
Am
bend,
my Huck - le - ber - ry
friend,
Moon
37
Dm7
G7
C
N.C.
Riv - er
and
me.
2.
41
C/E
Am
Dm7
G7
friend,
Moon
Riv - er
and
45
C
Fm
C
me.
rit. e dim.
p

CELEBRATE ME HOME

Lyrics by Kenny Loggins
Music By Kenny Loggins and Bob James
Arranged by Dan Coates

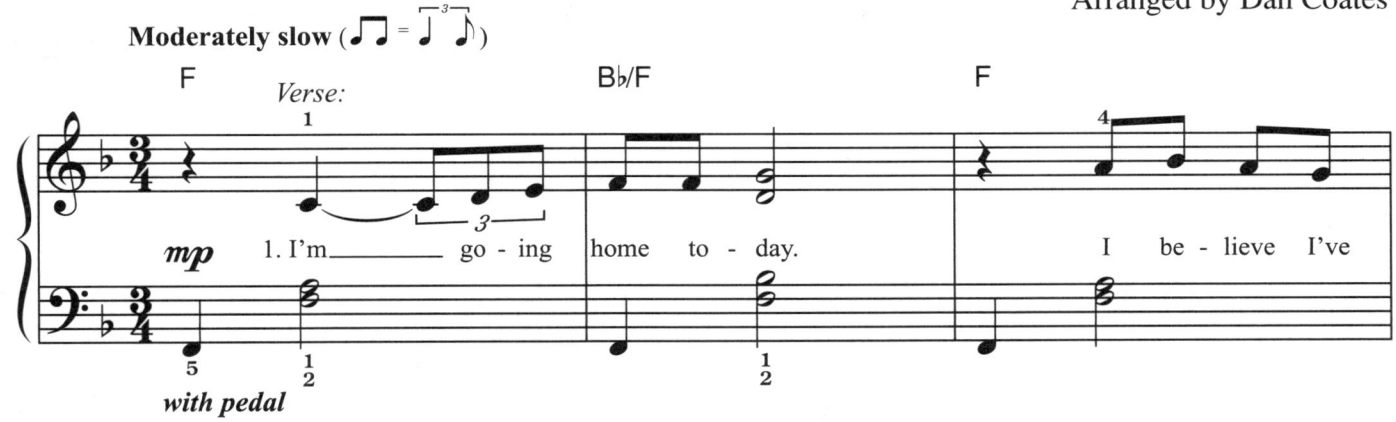

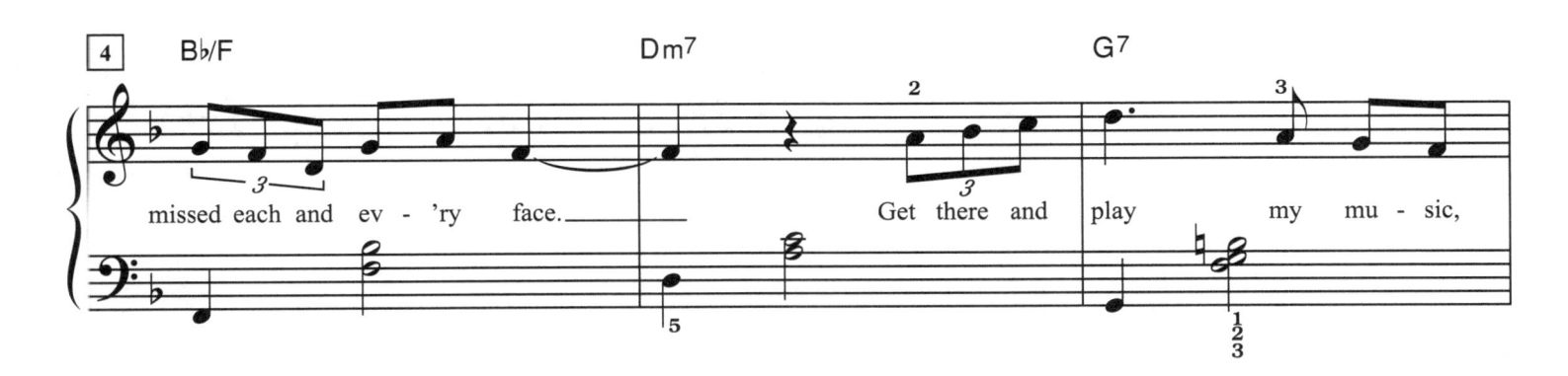

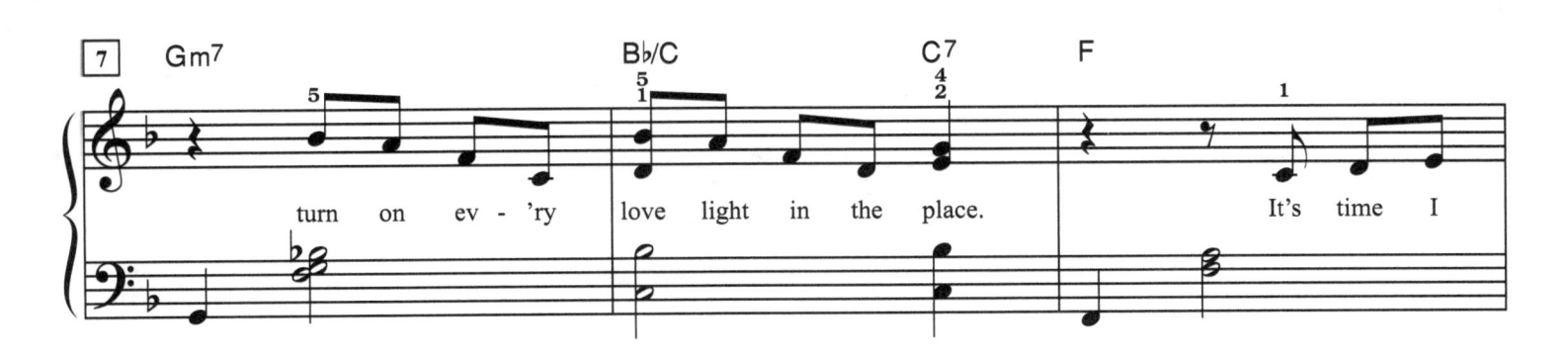

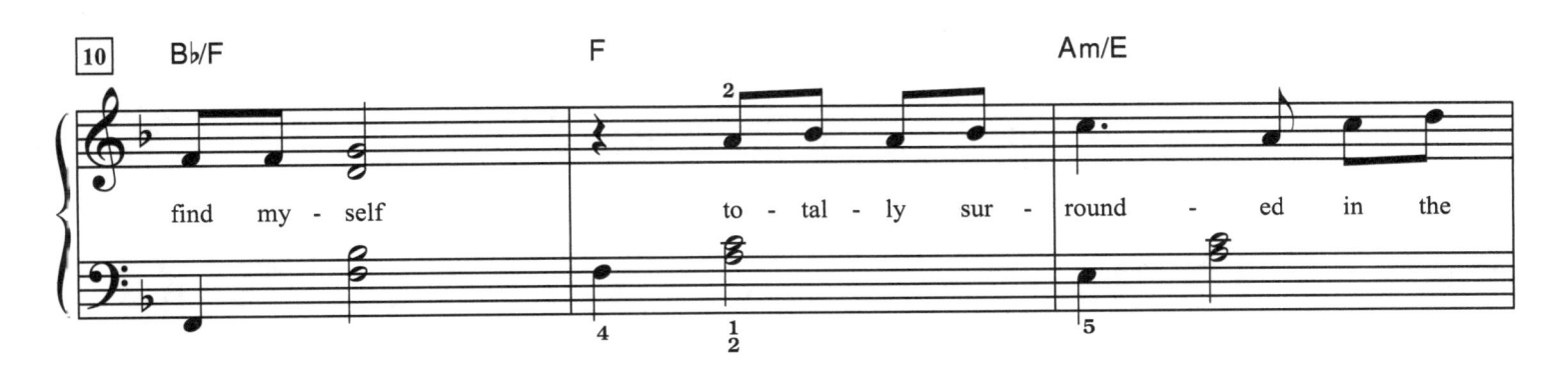

© 1977 (Renewed) MILK MONEY MUSIC
All Rights Reserved

13
Dm7
G7
Gm/C
C7
cir - cles
of
my
friends.
Chorus:
F
Am7
Dm7
Gm7
Please,
mf
cel - e - brate
me
home,
20
C7
A7/C♯
Dm7
Am7
Dm7
gim - me a num - ber.
Please,
cel - el - brate
me
23
Gm7
C7
B♭
Am7
home.
Play me one more
song
that I'll
al - ways re - mem - ber,

27
Dm
G7sus
G
Gm
and I can re - call when - ev - er I find my - self too all a -
30
C7
to Coda
F
F7
B♭/F
lone, I can sing me home.
dim.
34
E♭7
Verse:
F
B♭/F
F
2. Un - eas - y high - way, trav - 'lin' where the
mp
38
B♭/F
Dm7
G7
west - er - ly winds can fly. Some - bod - y tried to tell me,

32

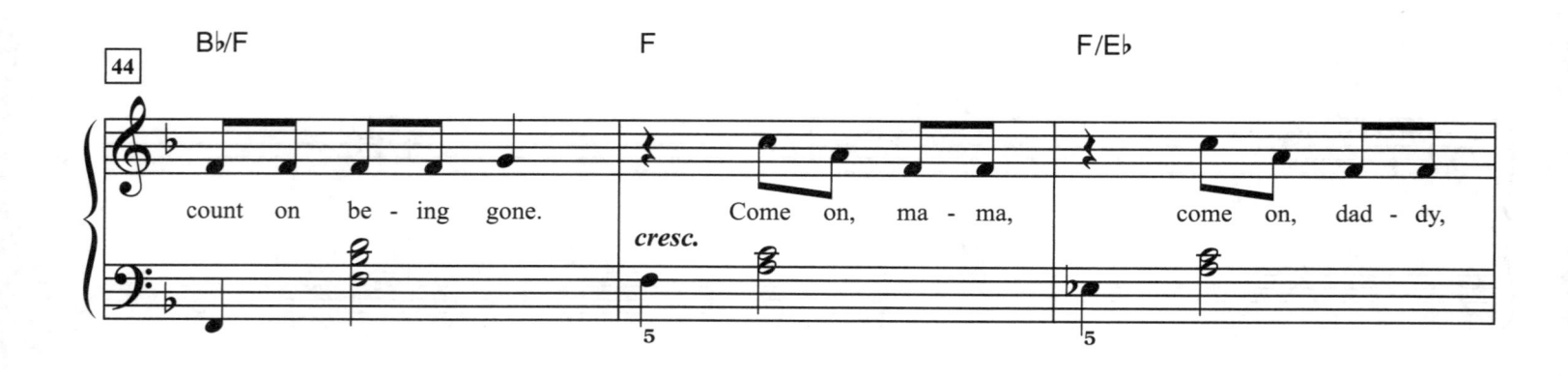

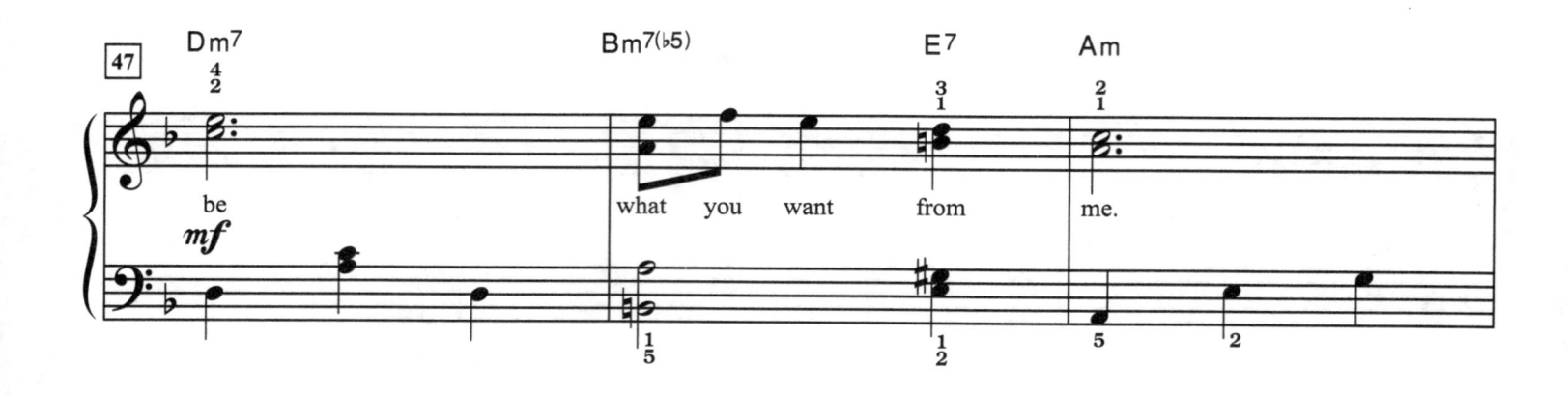

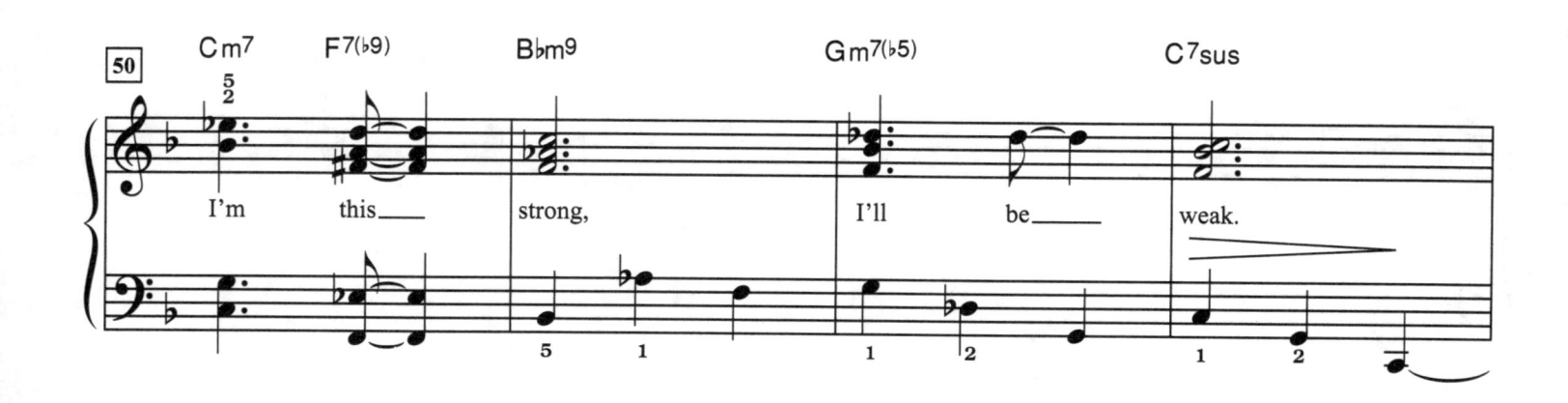

33

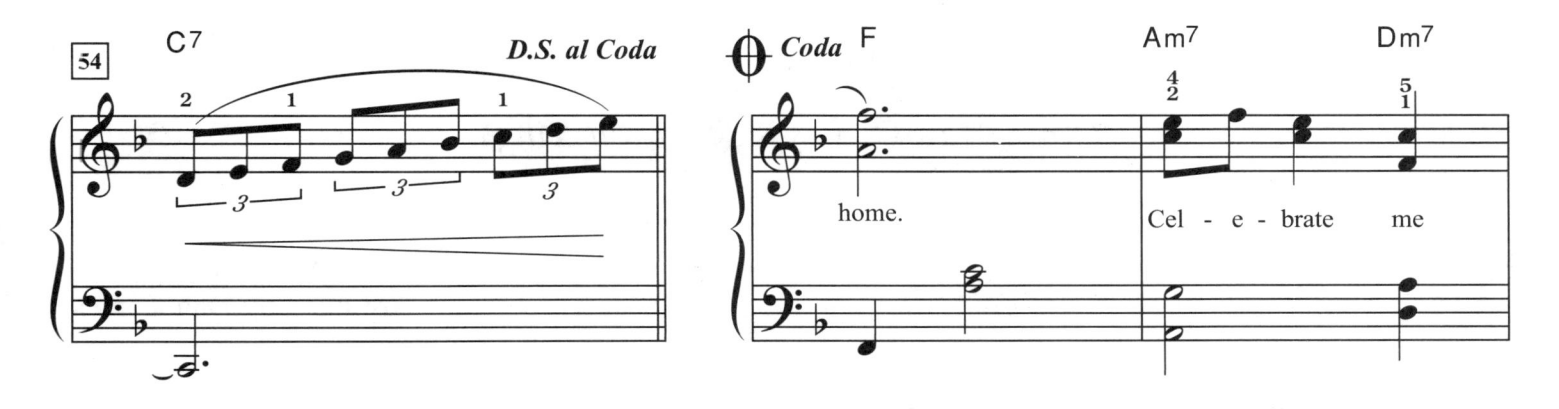

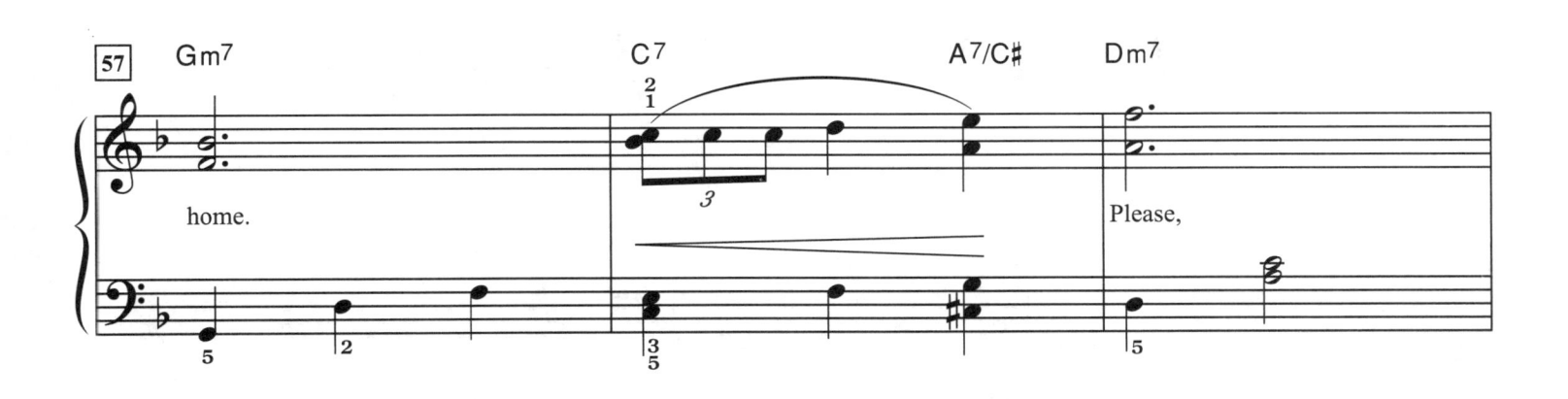

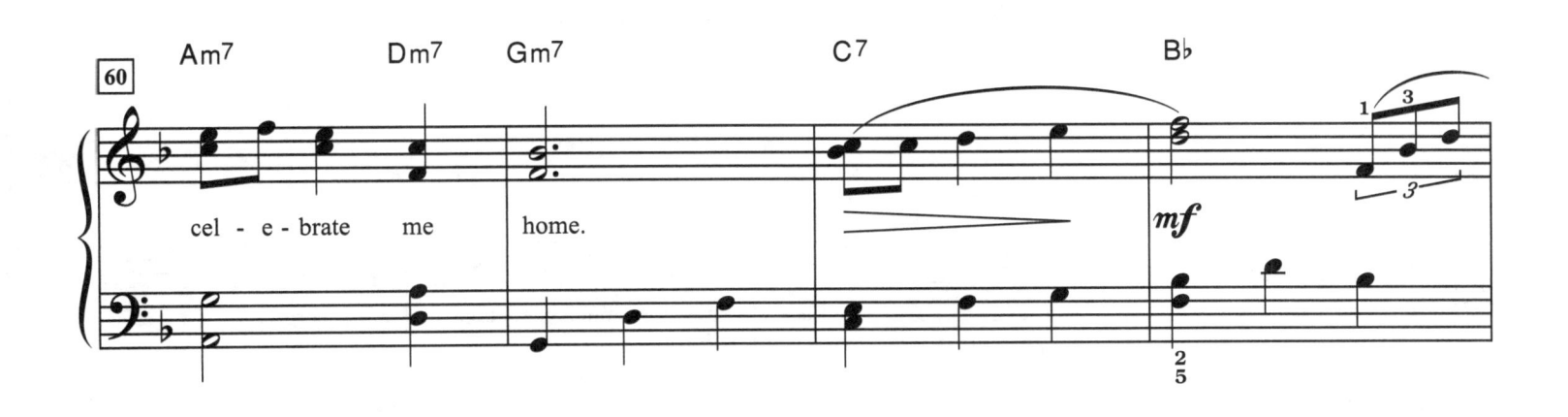

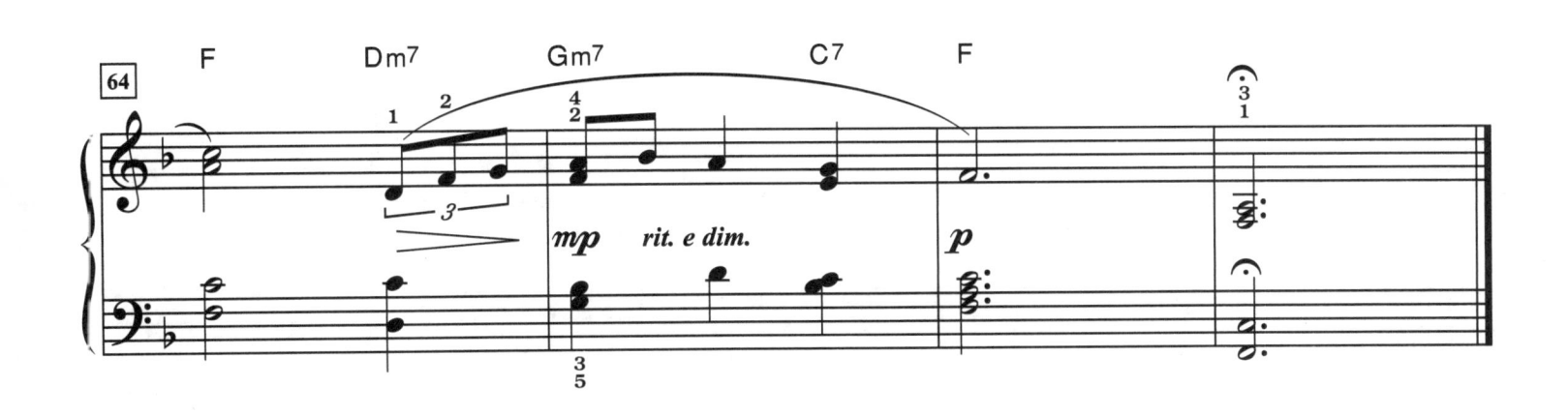

THE CIRCLE OF LIFE

(from Walt Disney's *The Lion King*)

Music by Elton John
Lyrics by Tim Rice
Arranged by Dan Coates

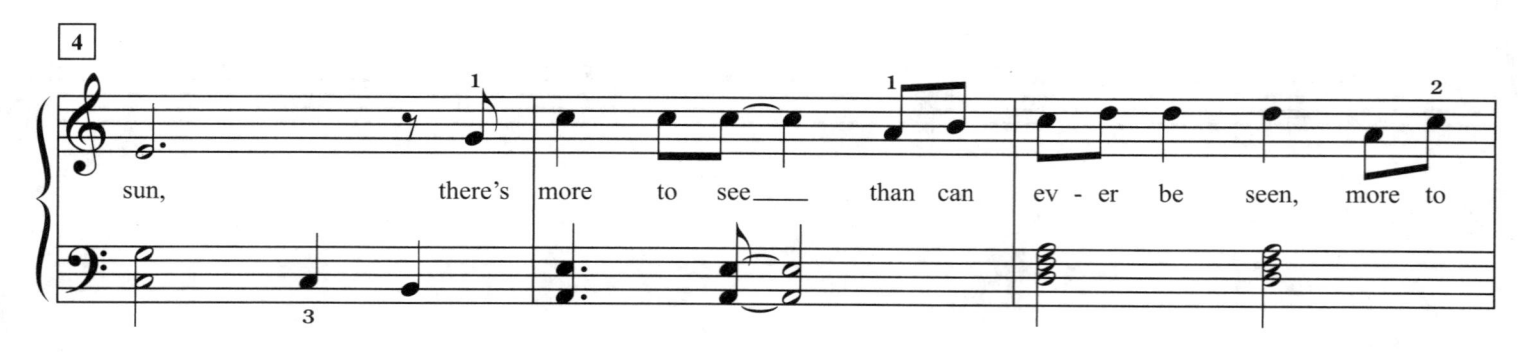

From the day we ar-rive on the plan-et and blink-ing, step in-to the sun, there's more to see than can ev-er be seen, more to do than can ev-er be done. There's far too much to take in here, more to find than can ev-er be found. But the sun roll-ing high through the

© 1994 WONDERLAND MUSIC COMPANY, INC.
All Rights Reserved

14
sap - phi - re sky keeps great and small on the end - less round. It's the cir - cle of
cresc.
17
life, and it moves us all through de - spair and
f
21
hope, through faith and love 'til we find our
25
place on the path un - wind - ing, in the
29
cir - cle, the cir - cle of life.
rit.
ff

DANCE WITH MY FATHER

Words and Music by
Luther Vandross and Richard Marx
Arranged by Dan Coates

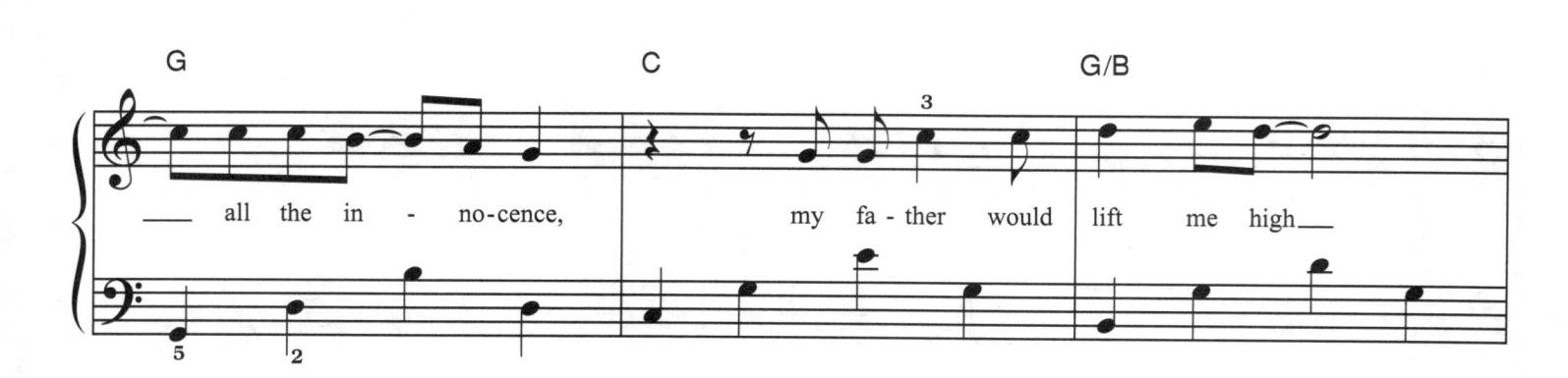

1. Back when I was a child,
2. *See additional lyrics*

be-fore life re-moved all the in-no-cence, my fa-ther would lift me high and dance with my moth-er and me and then spin me a-round till I fell

© 2002 UNCLE RONNIE'S MUSIC, INC., EMI APRIL MUSIC, INC. and CHI-BOY MUSIC
All Rights for CHI-BOY MUSIC outside the U.S. and Canada Administered by WB MUSIC CORP.
All Rights Reserved

15
F
Fm/A♭
C/G
D/F♯
a - sleep, then up the stairs he would car - ry me, and I knew for sure I was
19
G7sus
G7
Chorus:
C
G/B
Am
loved. If I could get an - oth - er chance, an - oth - er walk, an -
mf
23
F
Dm
Am
oth - er dance with him, I'd play a song that would nev - er, ev - er end. How I'd love,
26
F
G7sus
G7
1.
C
love, love to dance with my fa - ther a - gain.
mp
29
G/B
Am
F
2.
C
2. When
gain.
mp cresc.

33
F
G
C
G/B
Some-times, I'd lis - ten out - side her door,
and I'd hear how my moth - er cried
mf
36
Am
F
Gsus
G
Dm7
for him.
I pray for her e-ven more than me.
I pray for her e-ven more
dim.
40
Gsus
G
C
G/B
Am
than me.
p
45
F
C
G/B
Am
I
know I'm pray - ing for
much too much, but
could you send back the
mp
49
F
Dm
Am
on - ly man she loved?
I know you don't do it u - su - al - ly, but, dear Lord,
mf

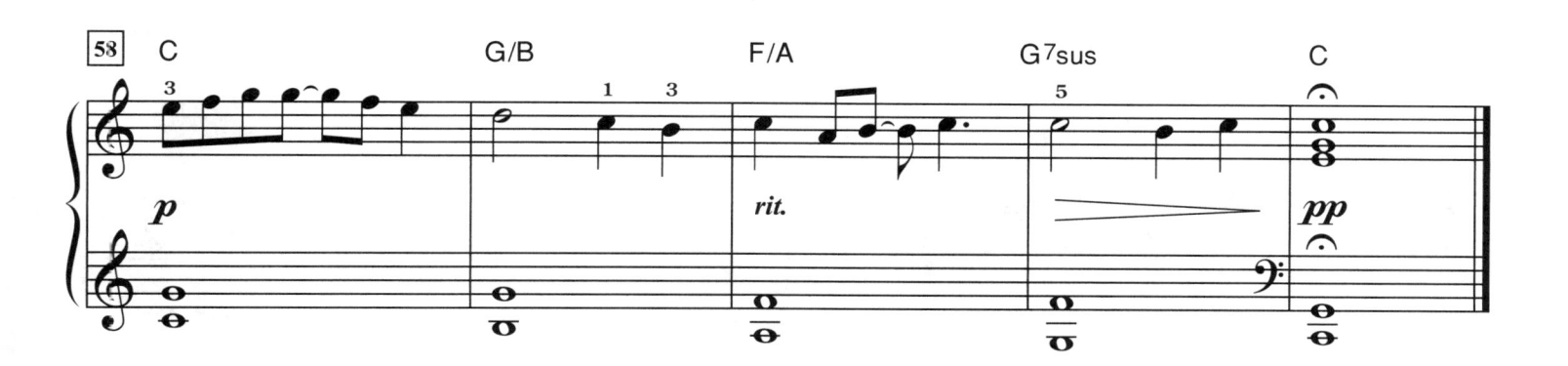

Verse 2:
When I and my mother would disagree,
To get my way, I would run from her to him.
He'd make me laugh just to comfort me,
Then finally make me do just what my mama said.
Later that night, when I was asleep,
He'd left a dollar under my sheet.
Never dreamed that would be gone from me.

Chorus 2:
If I could steal one final glance,
One final step,
One final dance with him,
I'd play a song that would never, ever end.
'Cause I'd love, love, love
To dance with my father again.

DESPERADO

Words and Music by
Don Henley and Glenn Frey
Arranged by Dan Coates

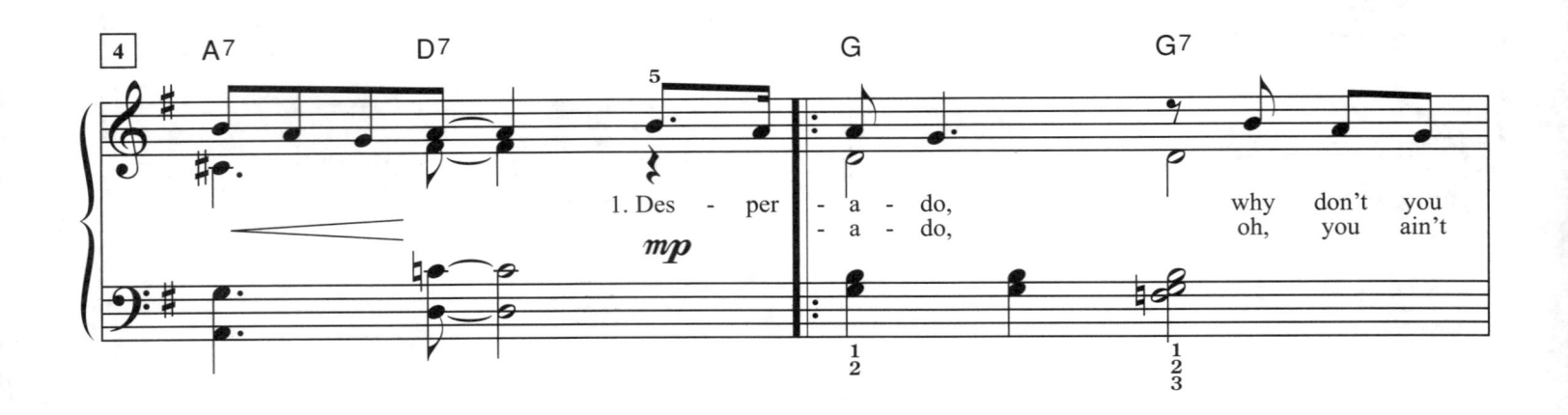

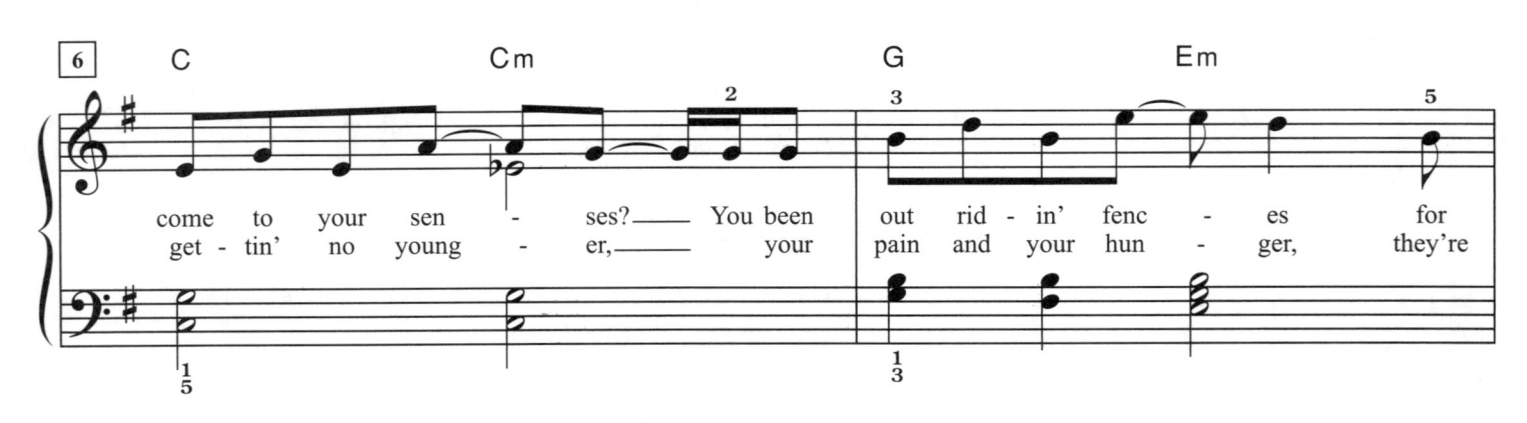

Slowly

with pedal

1. Des - per - a - do, why don't you come to your sen - ses? You been out rid - in' fenc - es for
   - a - do, oh, you ain't get - tin' no young - er, your pain and your hun - ger, they're

© 1973 (Renewed) CASS COUNTY MUSIC and RED CLOUD MUSIC
All Print Rights Administered by WARNER-TAMERLANE PUBLISHING CORP.
All Rights Reserved

8
A D7 G G7
so long now. Oh, you're a hard one, I know that
driv - ing you home. And free - dom, well, that's just
10
C Cm G/D B7/D♯ Em
you got your rea - sons, these things that are pleas - in' you can
some peo - ple talk - in', your pris - on is walk - in' through this
12
A7 D7 G D/F♯ Em Bm7
hurt you some - how. Don't you draw the queen of dia - monds, boy, she'll
world all a - lone. Don't your feet get cold in the win - ter - time? The
cresc.
mf
15
C G Em C
beat you if she's a - ble, you know the queen of hearts is al - ways your best
sky won't snow and the sun won't shine, it's hard to tell the night - time from the

17
G D/F♯ Em Bm7
bet. Now it seems to me some fine things have been
day. You're los - in' all your highs and lows. Ain't it
19
C G
1.
Em A7
laid up - on your ta - ble, but you on - ly want the ones that you can't
fun - ny how the feel - in' goes a -
21
Am7/D D7
2.
Am7 Am7/D D7
get. 2. Des - per way? Des - per -
mp
mp
24
G G7 C Cm G Em
a - do, why don't you come to your sens - es? Come down from your fenc - es,

27
A D7 G F/A G/B
o - pen the gate. It may be rain - in', but there's a
29
C Cm G Em G/D
rain - bow a - bove you. You bet - ter let some - bod - y - love you,
mf
31
C G/B Am7 G/D B7/D♯ Em
let some - bod - y love you, you bet - ter let some - bod - y love you be -
f
33
Am7/D D7 G G7 C Cm G
a tempo
fore it's too late.
rit.
mp
rit.
p

DON'T RAIN ON MY PARADE

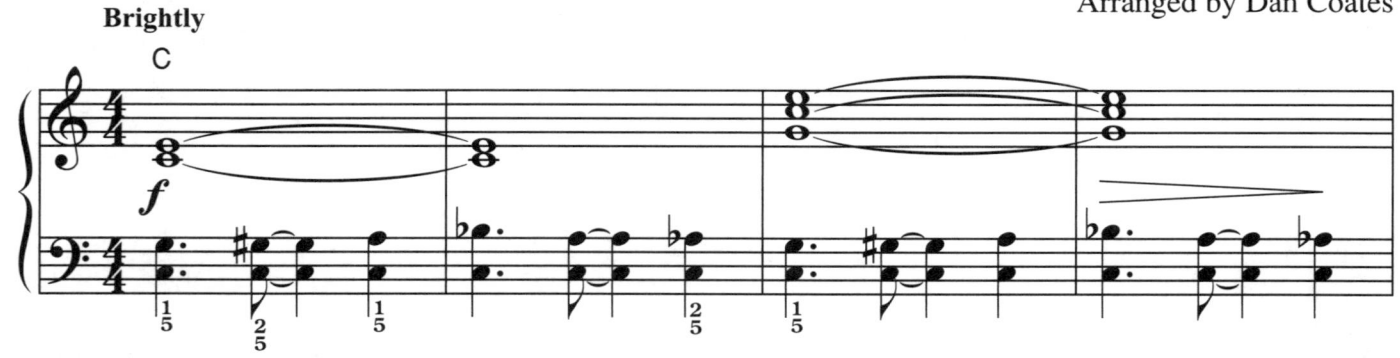

Music by Jule Styne
Words by Bob Merrill
Arranged by Dan Coates

© 1964 (Renewed) BOB MERRILL and JULE STYNE
Publication and Allied Rights Assigned to WONDERFUL MUSIC, INC.
and Administered by CHAPPELL & CO.
All Rights Reserved

15
F Dm7 Gm7 C7 F Fm
band out, I'll beat my drum. And if I'm
f
19
C Gm7 A Dm7(♭5)
fanned out, your turn at bat, sir, at least I did-n't fake it.
23
G7 C
Hat, sir, I guess I did-n't make it! But wheth - er I'm the
mf
26
rose of sheer per-fec-tion or freck - le on the nose of life's com-plex-ion,

29
Dm
G7
Em7sus
A7
the cin - der or the shin-y ap-ple of its eye,
33
D
Fm
C
Cdim
G7
Cmaj7
C7
I got - ta fly once, I got - ta try once, on - ly can die once, right sir?
f
37
D
Fm
C
Cdim
B7
Em
Dm7
G7
Ooh, love is juic - y, juic - y and you see I got-ta have my bite, sir.
41
C
mf
Get read - y for me, love, 'cause I'm a "com-er," I sim - ply got - ta

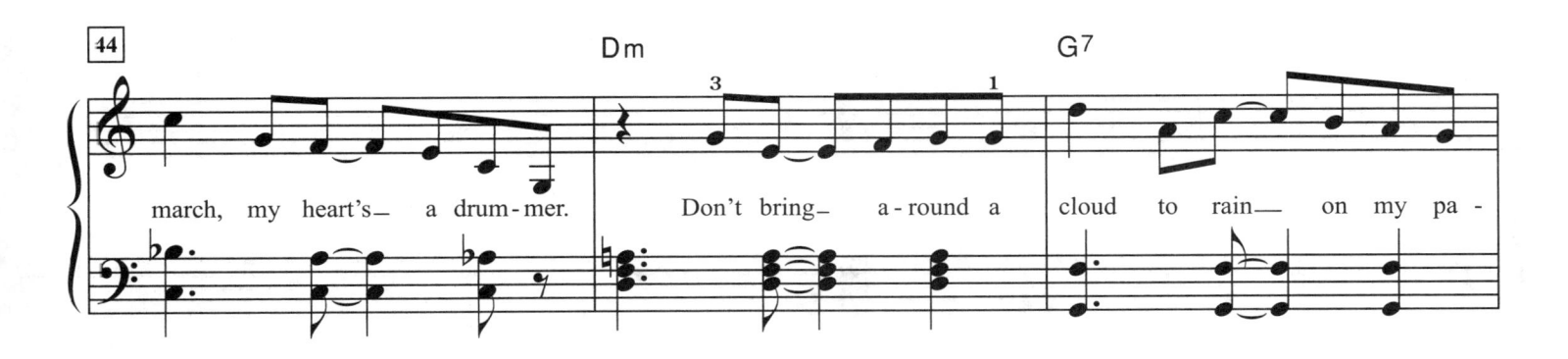

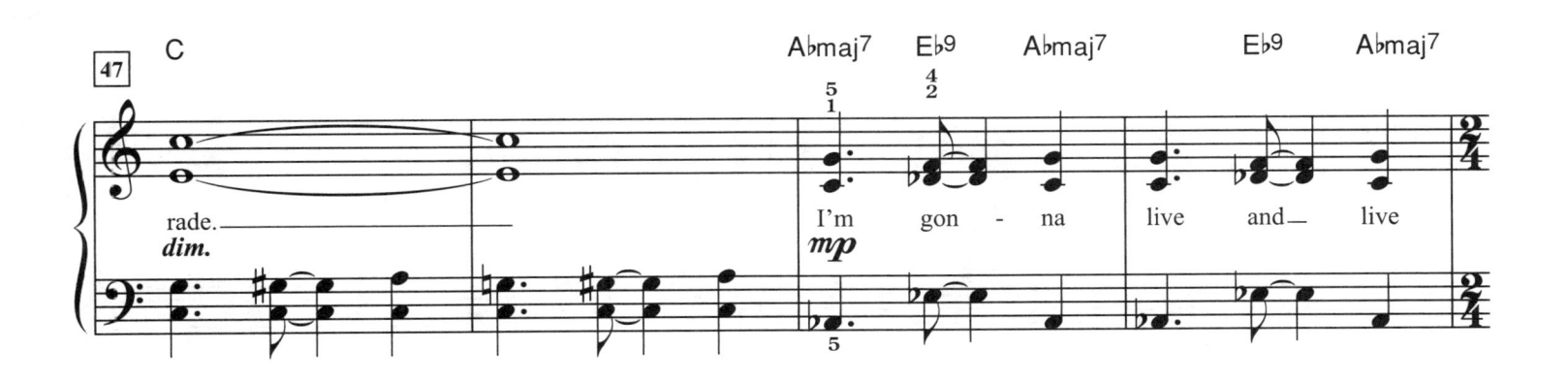

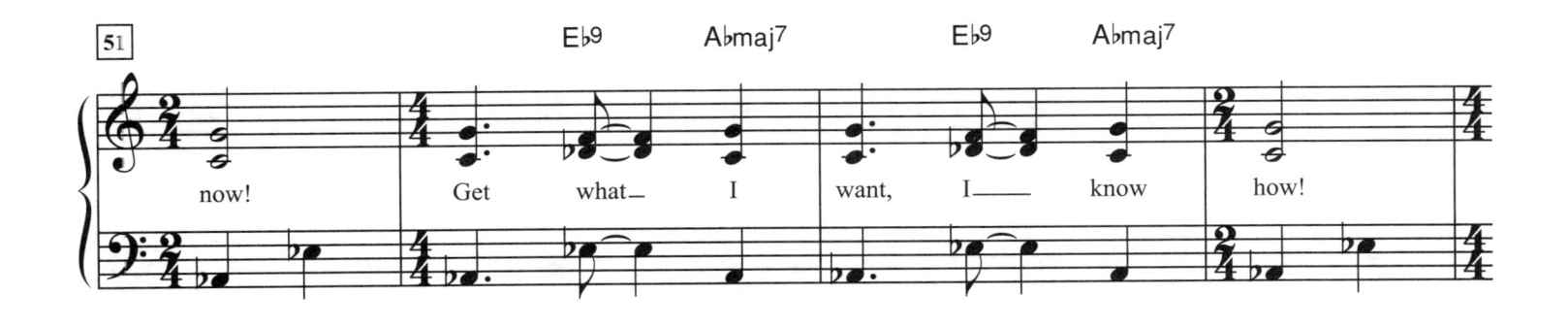

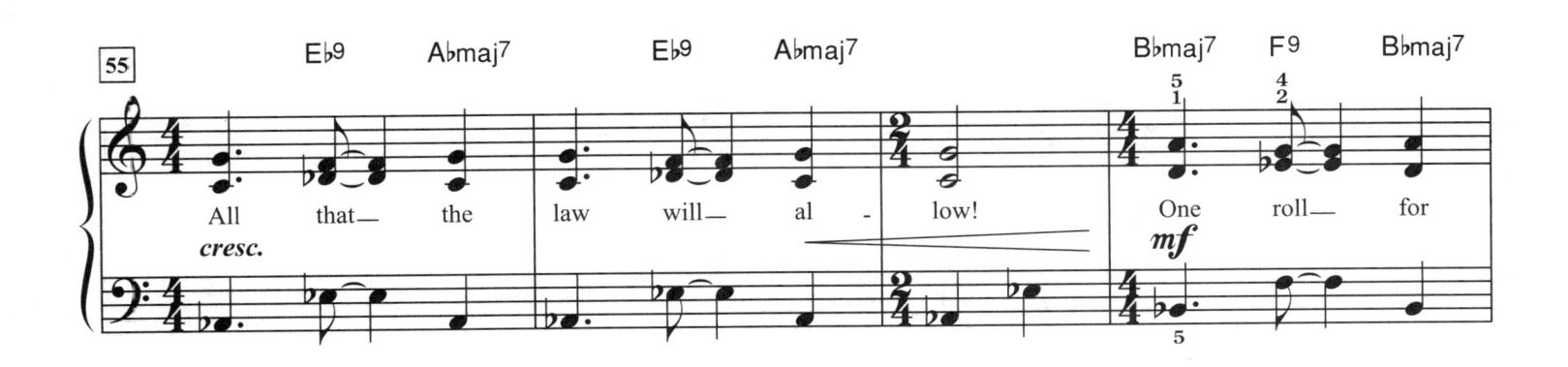

march, my heart's a drum-mer. Don't bring a-round a cloud to rain on my pa-rade. I'm gon-na live and live now! Get what I want, I know how! All that the law will al-low! One roll for

59
F9 B♭maj7 F9 B♭maj7 F9 B♭maj7
the whole_ she - bang! One throw,_ that bell will_ go
63
F9 B♭maj7 F9 B♭maj7
clang! Though I'm_ a - lone I'm_ a gang!
cresc.
67
Cmaj7 G9 Cmaj7 G9 Cmaj7
Eye on_ the tar - get_ and wham!
f
70
Cmaj7 G9 Cmaj7 G9 Cmaj7 F/G E/G
One shot,_ one gun shot_ and bam! Hey world,
ff
3

74
F/G E/G F/G C
here I am! Get ready for me
f
78
D♭
love, 'cause I'm a "com-er," I sim-ply got-ta march, my heart's a drum-mer.
cresc.
81
C/G Am7 Dm Em Fmaj7 D♭maj7
No-bod-y, no, no-bod-y is gon-na rain on my pa-
ff
meno mosso
85
C
rade!
fff a tempo
sfz
RH
LH

8TH WORLD WONDER

Words and Music by
Kyle Jacobs, Shaun Shankel
and Joel Parkes
Arranged by Dan Coates

With a moderate, steady beat

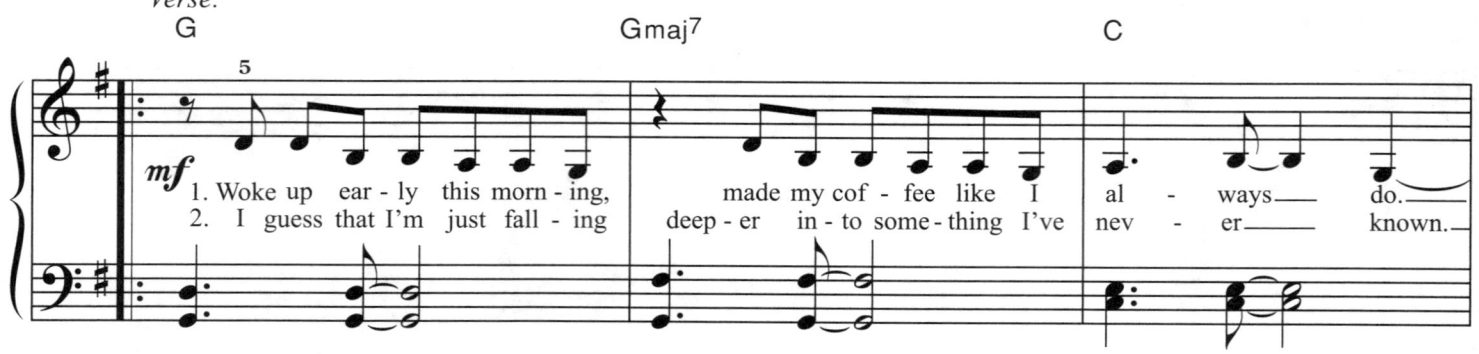

Verse:

1. Woke up early this morning, made my coffee like I always do.
2. I guess that I'm just falling deeper into something I've never known.

Then it hit me from nowhere, ev'rything I feel about
But the way that I'm feeling makes me realize that it

me and you.
can't be wrong.

The way you
Your love's like a

© 2002, 2004 CURB SONGS (ASCAP)/JACOBSONG (Administered by CURB SONGS) (ASCAP)/
SHANKEL SONGS (ASCAP)/BEEBOP MUSIC, a division of BBC WORLDWIDE LTD. (SOCAN)
All Rights Reserved

14
C D Em C D
kiss me cra - zy. Ba - by, you're so a - maz - ing.
sum - mer rain, cresc. wash - ing my doubts a - way.
Chorus:
17
G D Em
f
Sev - en days and sev - en nights of thun - der. The wa - ter's ris - ing and I'm
20
C G D
slip - ping un - der. I think I fell in love with the eighth world won -
23
Em 1. C
der. Yeah, yeah, yeah.

2.
Bridge:
26
C
Em
C D
Yeah, yeah, yeah.
It's on - ly been a week but,
it's com - ing o - ver me, yeah.
mf
29
Em
C D
G
It's mak - ing me be - lieve that
you're the one for me.
f
32
D
Em
C
35
G
D
Em
mf
cresc.

Chorus:
38
C D G D
Sev - en days and sev - en nights of thun - der.
41
Em C G
The wa - ter's ris - ing and I'm slip - ping un - der. I think I fell in love
44
D Em
1., 2.
C
with the eighth world won - der. Yeah, yeah, yeah, yeah.
47
3.
C G D
Hey, yeah, hey, oh,
mf
50
Em C G
yeah.
rit. e dim.
mp

IF EVER I WOULD LEAVE YOU

Music by Frederick Loewe
Lyrics by Alan Jay Lerner
Arranged by Dan Coates

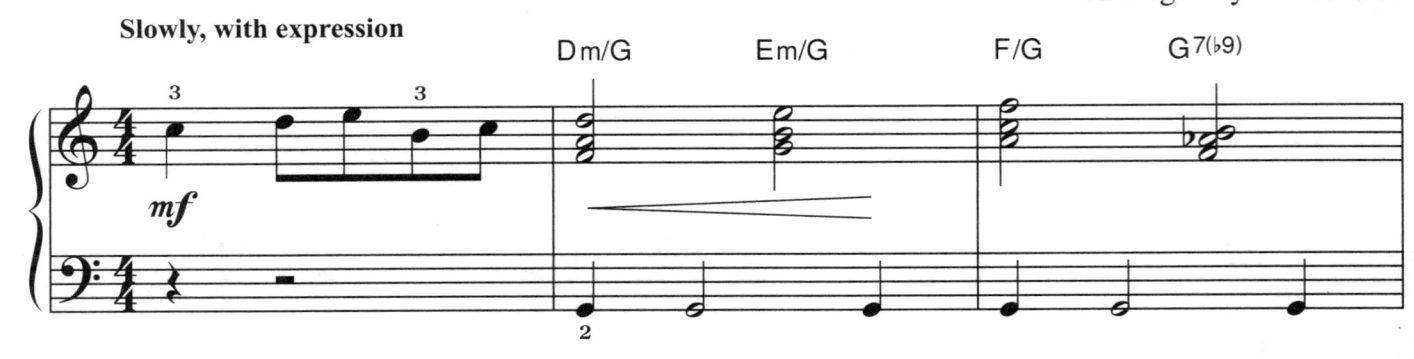

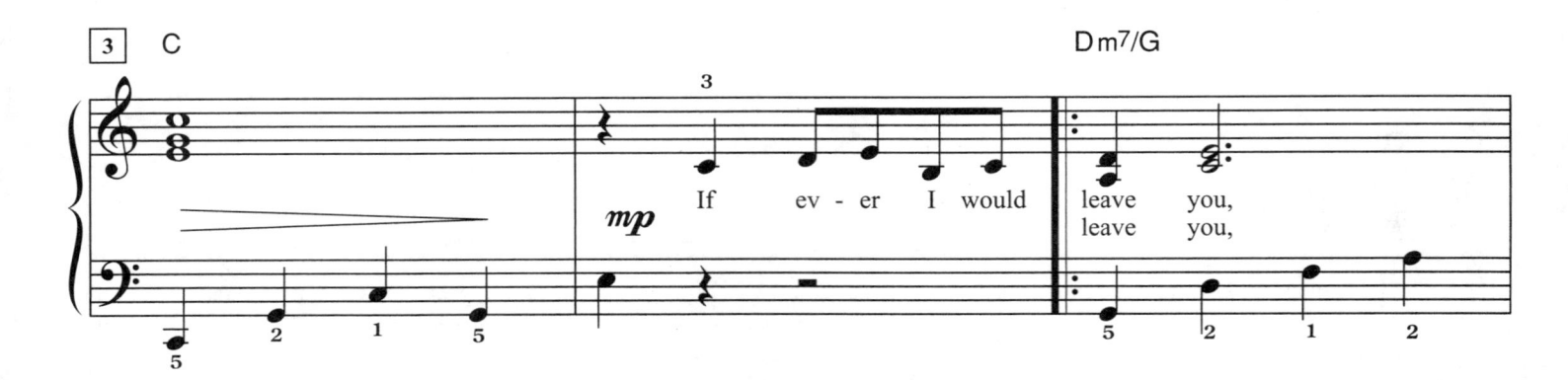

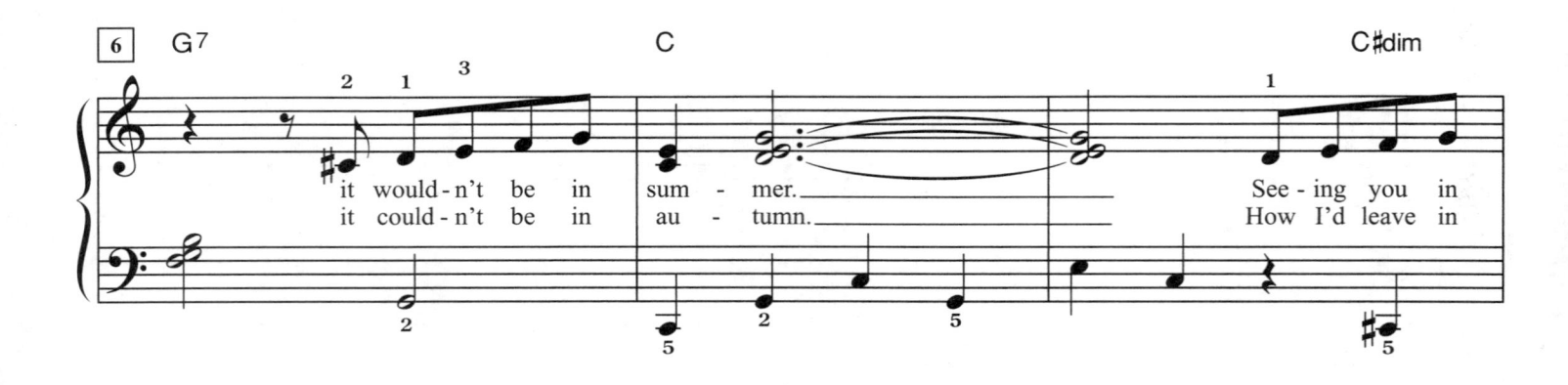

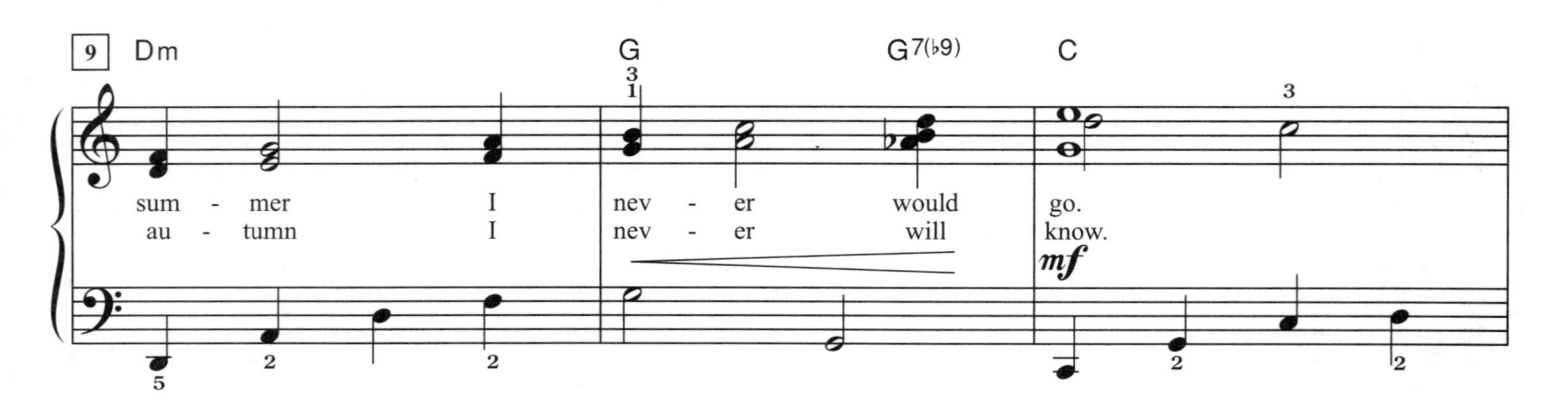

If ever I would leave you,
it wouldn't be in summer.
Seeing you in summer I never would go.

it couldn't be in autumn.
How I'd leave in autumn I never will know.

© 1960 (Renewed) by ALAN JAY LERNER and FREDERICK LOEWE
Publication and Allied Rights Assigned to CHAPPELL & CO., INC.
All Rights Reserved

12 Cmaj7 C7 Fmaj7 Dm G7
Your hair streaked with sun - light, your lips red as
I've seen how you spar - kle when fall nips the
15 Cmaj7 Am7 Dm Dm(maj7)
flame, your face with a lus - tre
air. I know you in au - tumn
1.
18 Dm7 Dm7/G G N.C.
that puts gold to shame. But if I'd ev - er
mp
2.
21 Dm7 G7 C
and I must be there. And could I
mp

24
E
F♯m7
B
E
leave you run - ning merr - 'ly through the snow?
27
A♭
F♯m7
B7
Or on a win - try eve - ning when you catch the fi - re's
cresc.
30
E
G7
Dm7/G
glow? If ev - er I would leave you,
mf
33
G7
C
C♯dim
how could it be in spring - time, know-ing how in

36
Dm
G
G7(♭9)
C
Cmaj7
C7
spring I'm be - witched by you so? Oh, no! Not in
f
40
F
Fmaj7
Dm7
Fm
C/G
spring - time, sum - mer, win - ter or fall!
43
D7
N.C.
Dm7/G
G7(♭9)
No, nev - er could I leave you at
sf
mf
46
C
D♭
C
all!
f
rit.
ff

INSIDE YOUR HEAVEN

Words and Music by
Andreas Carlsson, Per Nylen and Savan Kotecha
Arranged by Dan Coates

Slowly

with pedal

Verse:

1. I've been down, now I'm blessed. Felt a rev-e-la-tion com-in' 'round. Guess it's right, it's so a- maz-ing. Ev-'ry-time I see you, I'm a-live. You're all I

© 2005 WB MUSIC CORP., ANDREAS CARLSSON PUBLISHING AB,
UNIVERSAL MUSIC PUBLISHING AB and OH SUKI MUSIC
All Rights for itself and ANDREAS CARLSSON PUBLISHING AB Administered by WB MUSIC CORP.
All Rights Reserved

13
Am D Am7 G/B
got. You lift me up. The sun and the moon-light, all my
16
C Dsus D
Chorus:
G
dreams are in your eyes. And I wan-na be in-side your
mf
18
C G/B Am7 G/B
heav - en. Take me to the place you cry from, when a
20
C Dsus D G
storm blows you a - way. I wan-na be the earth that
22
C G/B Am7 G/B
holds you, ev - 'ry bit of air you're breath - in' in, a sooth - in' wind. I
f

24
C Dsus D G G/B C
wan - na be in - side your heav - en.
dim.
2. When we
27
Verse:
G C/G G
touch, when we love, the stars line up, a wrong be-comes un -
mp
30
C/G Em F C
done. Nat - 'ral - ly, my soul sur - ren - ders. The sun and the
33
Am7 G/B C Dsus D
Chorus:
G
moon - light, all my dreams are in your arms. And I wan - na be in - side your
cresc.
mf
36
C G/B Am7 G/B
heav - en. Take me to the place you cry from, when a

38
C Dsus D G
storm blows you a - way. And I wan-na be the earth that
40
C G/B Am7 G/B
holds you, ev-'ry bit of air you're breath-in' in, a sooth - in' wind. I
f
42
to Coda
C Dsus D G
wan-na be in - side your heav-en. When
mf
Bridge:
C G/B
min-utes turn to days and years, if
45
Am7 D C G/B Dsus
D.S. al Coda
D
moun-tains fall, I'd still be here hold-ing you un - til the day I die.
f
Coda
Em G/D C Dsus D G
heav - en.
mf
rit. e dim.
mp

MUSIC OF MY HEART

Words and Music by
Diane Warren
Arranged by Dan Coates

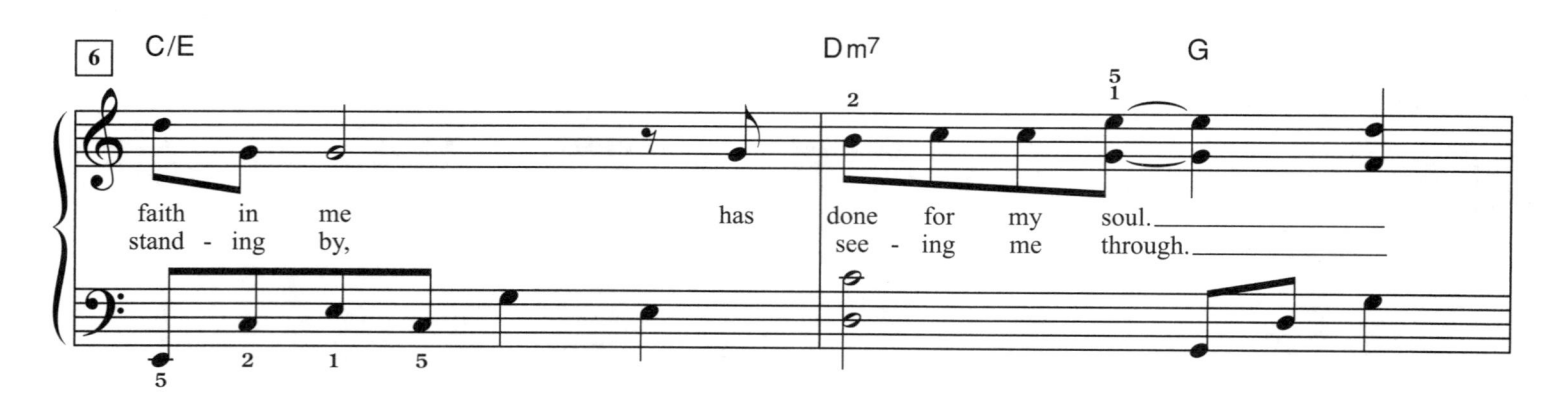

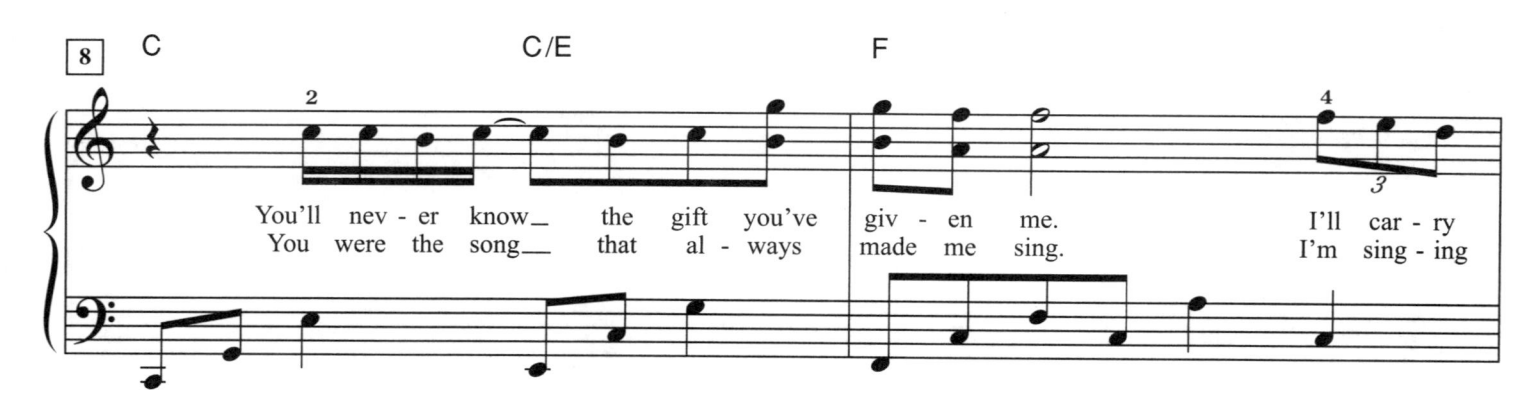

Slowly, with feeling

with pedal

Verse:

1. You'll nev-er know_____ what you've done for me,_____ what your
2. You were the one_____ al-ways on my side,_____ al-ways

faith in me_____ has done for my soul._____
stand-ing by,_____ see-ing me through._____

You'll nev-er know___ the gift you've giv-en me. I'll car-ry
You were the song___ that al-ways made me sing. I'm sing-ing

© 1991 REALSONGS (ASCAP)
All Rights Reserved

10
C/E
Dm7
it with me.
this for you.
Through the days a - head, I
Ev - 'ry - where I go, I
12
C/E
B♭
think of days be - fore, when you made me
think of where I've been and of the
hope for some - thing bet - ter and made me
one who knew me bet - ter than an - y - one
Chorus:
14
Dm7/G
G7
C
G/B
reach for some - thing more.
ev - er will a - gain.
You taught me to
run, you taught me to fly, helped me to
mf
16
Dm7
F
C/E
free the me in - side. Helped me hear the
mu - sic of my heart. Helped me hear the

18
Dm7 G7 C G/B
mu - sic of my heart. You o-pened my eyes, you o-pened the door to some-thing I've
20
B♭maj7
to Coda
1.
Dm7 Dm7/G B♭sus2
nev-er known be-fore. And your love is the mu-sic of my heart.
mp
2.
Bridge:
23
Dm7 Dm7/G F G
love is the mu - sic of my heart. What you taught me, on - ly
mp
mf
25
F/A G/B
your love could ev - er teach me. You got through where no one could reach me be - fore.

27
C
Dm7
'Cause you al - ways saw in me all the
29
C/E
B♭maj7
Dm7/G
D.S. al Coda
best that I could be. It was you who set me free. You taught me to
cresc.
Coda
Dm7
Dm7/G
B♭sus2
love is the mu - sic of my heart,
33
F/G
G7
C
is the mu - sic of my heart.
rit. e dim.
p

(I CAN'T GET NO) SATISFACTION

Words and Music by
Mick Jagger and Keith Richards
Arranged by Dan Coates

Moderately, with a steady rock beat

13
F
C7
F
and I try
and I try
and I try.
cresc.
16
B♭
F
E♭/B♭
B♭
I can't
get no,
I can't
f
19
F
E♭/B♭
B♭
Verse:
F
get no...
1. When I'm
2., 3. See additional lyrics.
driv - in' in my car
22
E♭/B♭
B♭
F
E♭/B♭
B♭
and the
man comes on the ra - di - o; he's

25
F Eb/Bb Bb F
tell - in' me more and more___ a - bout some___ use - less in - for - ma -
28
Eb/Bb Bb F Eb/Bb Bb
2
tion sup - posed to fire my im - ag - i - na - tion. I can't
31
F Eb/Bb Bb F
1
get no... Oh, no, no, no.
34
F Eb/Bb Bb
5 1 5
Hey, hey, hey.___ That's what I say.___
f

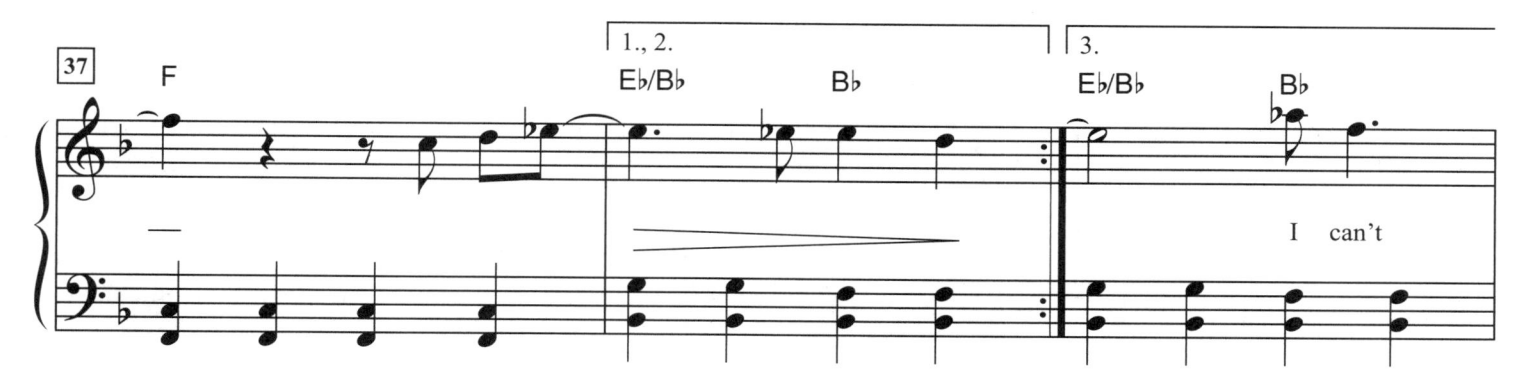

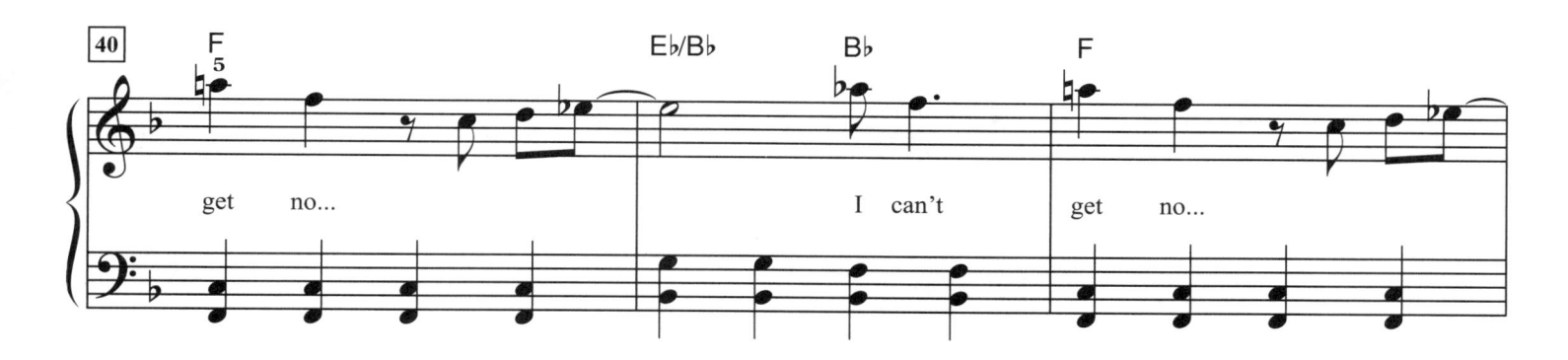

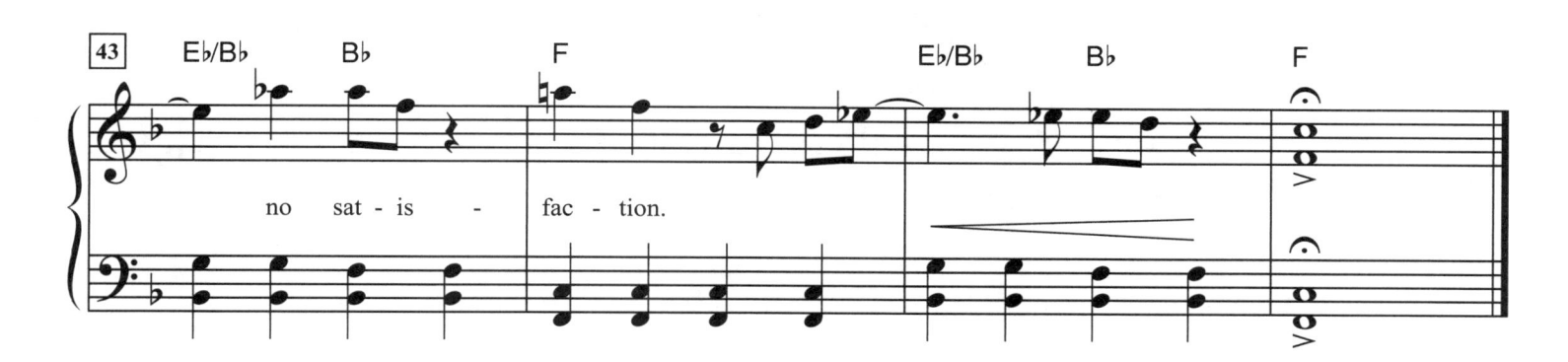

Verse 2:
When I'm watchin' my T.V.
And a man comes on and tells me
How white my shirts can be.
But, he can't be a man
'Cause he doesn't smoke the same cigarettes as me.
I can't get no,
Oh, no, no, no.

Verse 3:
When I'm ridin' 'round the world,
And I'm doin' this and I'm signin' that,
And I'm tryin' to make some girl,
Who tells me, baby, better come back maybe next week.
'Cause you see I'm on a losin' streak.
I can't get no,
Oh, no, no, no.

SUMMERTIME

Music and Lyrics by George Gershwin,
Du Bose and Dorothy Heyward and Ira Gershwin
Arranged by Dan Coates

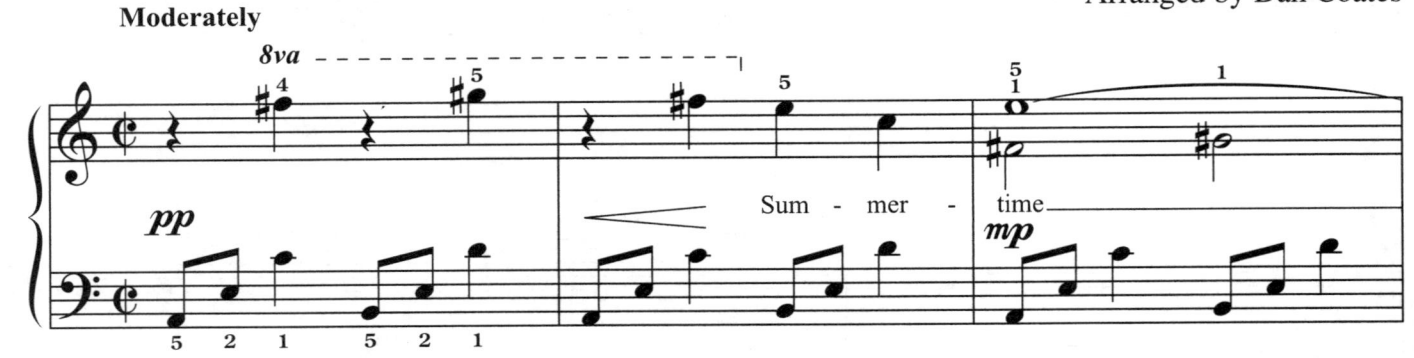

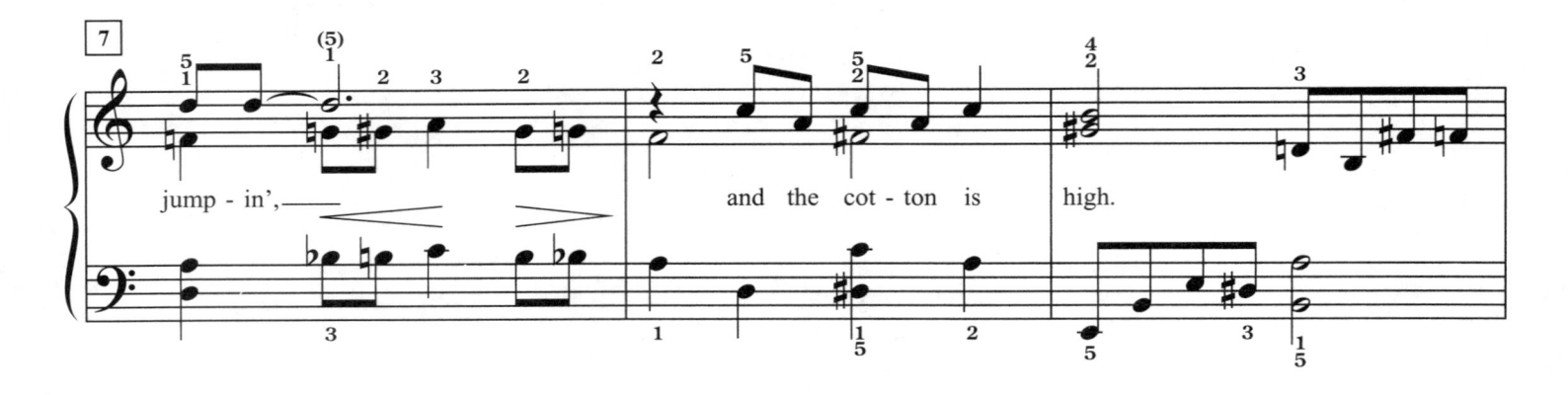

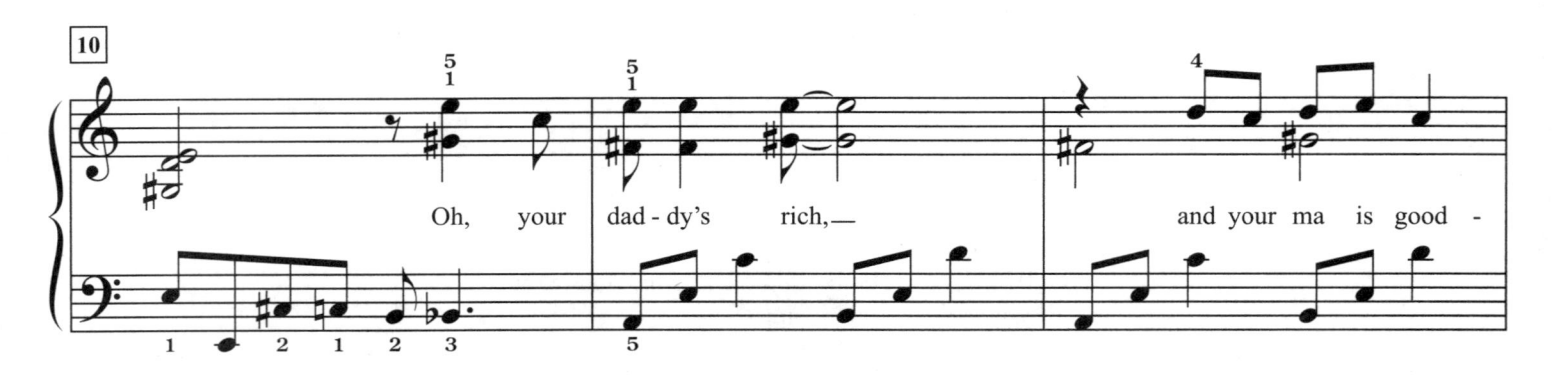

Moderately

Sum - mer - time and the liv - in' is eas - y, Fish are jump - in', and the cot - ton is high. Oh, your dad - dy's rich, and your ma is good -

© 1935 (Renewed) GEORGE GERSHWIN MUSIC, IRA GERSHWIN MUSIC and
DU BOSE AND DOROTHY HEYWARD MEMORIAL FUND
All Rights Administered by WB MUSIC CORP.
All Rights Reserved

71

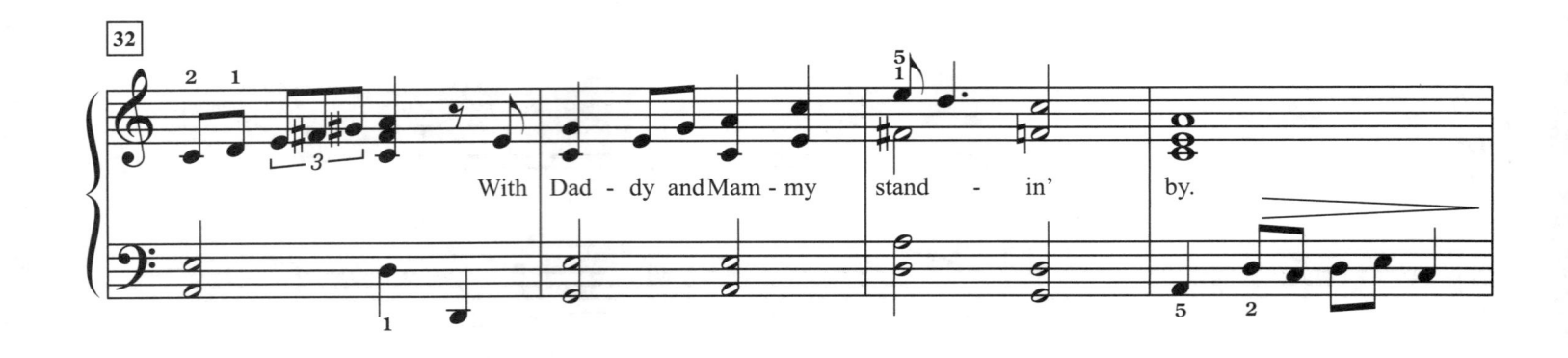

and you'll take to the sky. But till that mornin' there's a nothin' can harm you With Daddy and Mammy standin' by.

A WHOLE NEW WORLD
(from Walt Disney's *Aladdin*)

Words by Tim Rice
Music by Alan Menken
Arranged by Dan Coates

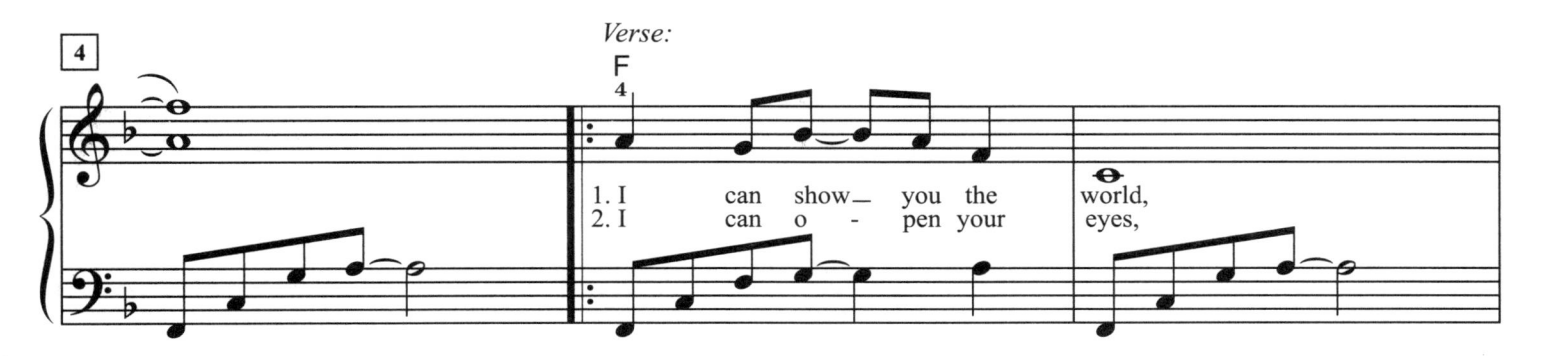

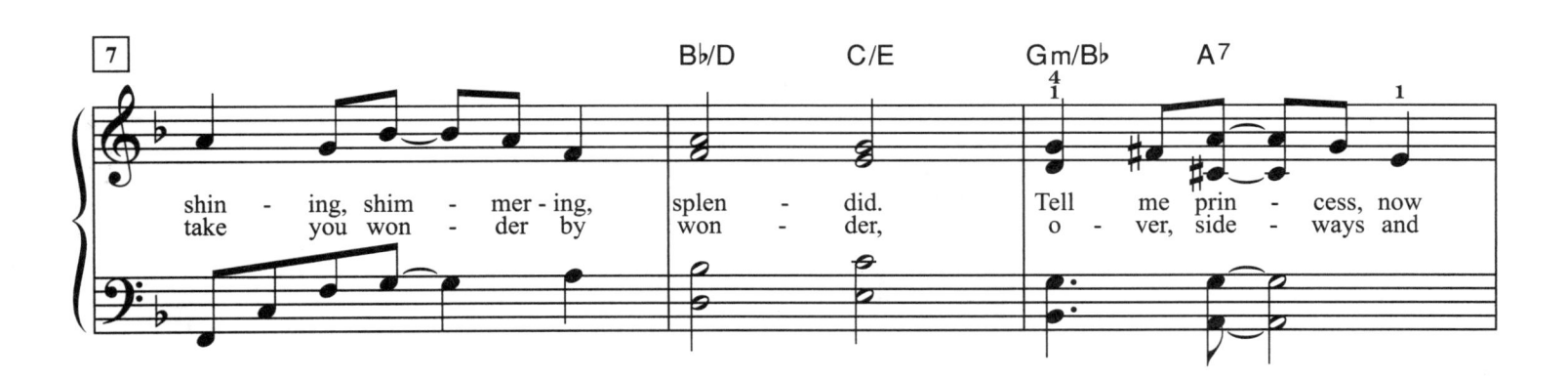

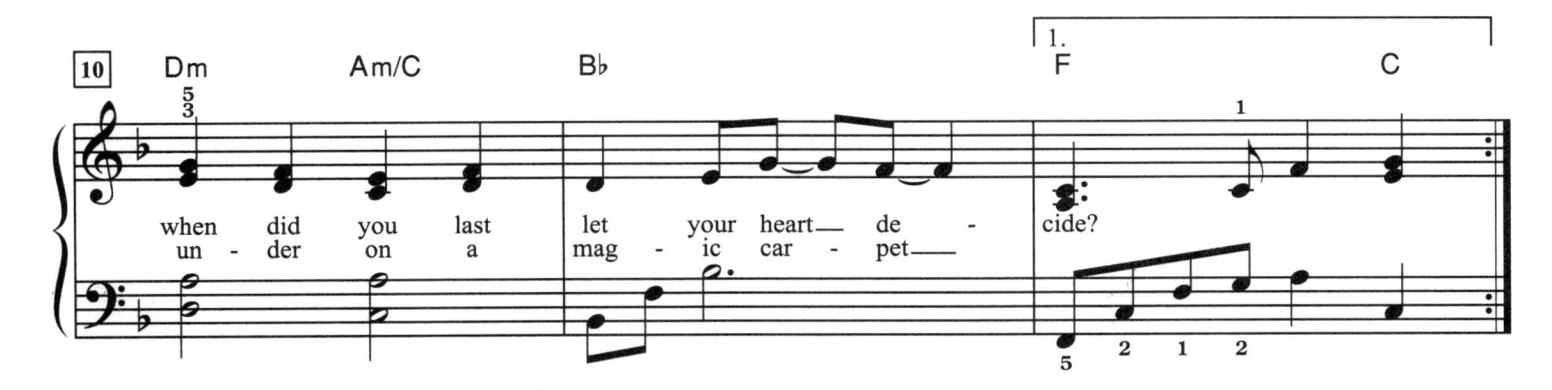

Moderately, with expression

mp legato
with pedal

Verse:

1. I can show you the world, shining, shimmering, splendid. Tell me princess, now when did you last let your heart de- cide?
2. I can o- pen your eyes, take you wonder by wonder, o- ver, sideways and un- der on a mag- ic car- pet

© 1992 WONDERLAND MUSIC COMPANY, INC. and WALT DISNEY MUSIC COMPANY
All Rights Reserved   Used by Permission

2.
Chorus:
13
F Gm/F C F Gm/F
ride. A whole new world, a new fan -
mf
16
C C7/E F Bb F/A
tas - tic point of view. No one to tell us no or
3
19
Bb F/A Dm7 G7 Bb/C
where to go or say we're on - ly dream - ing. A whole new
22
C F Gm/F C C#dim
world, a daz - zling place I nev - er
f

25
Dm F7 B♭ F/A B♭ F/A
knew. But when I'm way up here it's cry - stal clear that
28
Dm7 G7sus G E♭ B♭/C Dm
now I'm in a whole new world with you.
mf
31
F/C B♭(add 9) F/C
A whole new world, that's where we'll
34
Gm7 F/A B♭(add 9)
be. A thrill - ing chase, a won - d'rous
37
B♭/C F F(add 9)
place, for you and me.
mp rit. e dim.
p

WEEKEND IN NEW ENGLAND

Words and Music by Randy Edelman
Arranged by Dan Coates

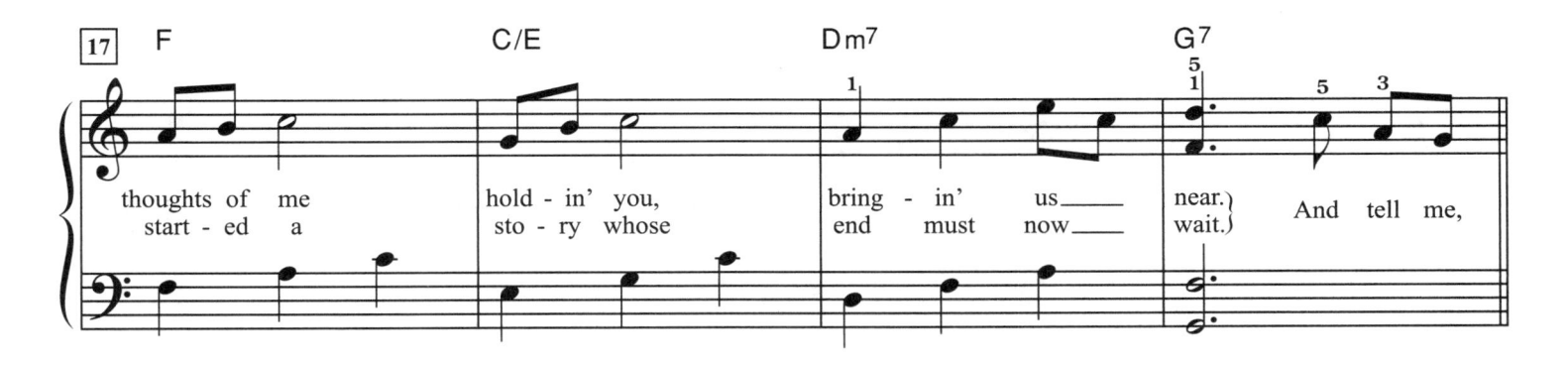

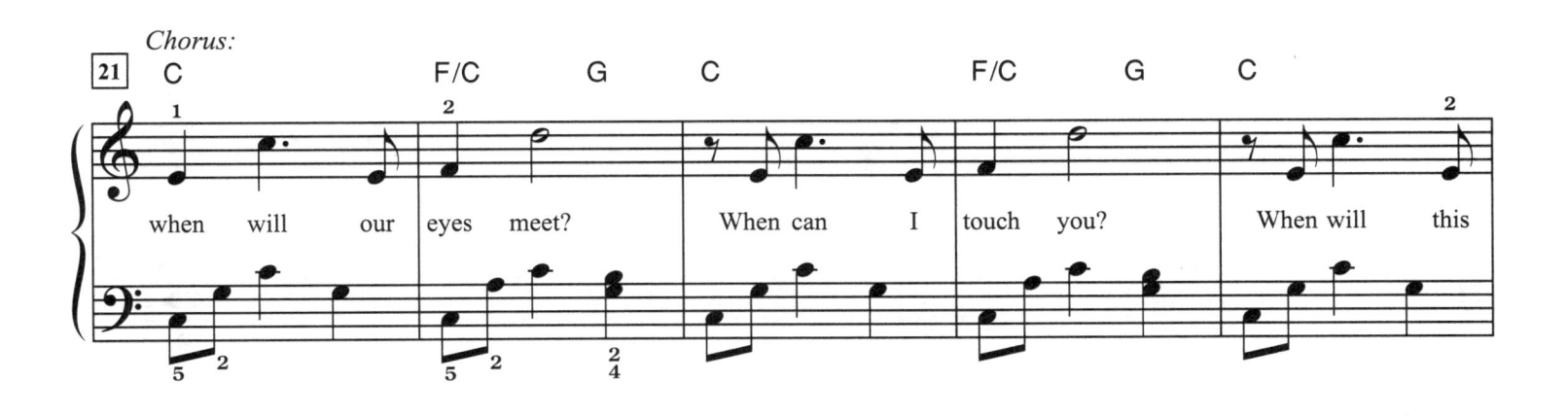

77

thoughts of me / start-ed a | hold-in' you, / sto-ry whose | bring-in' us near. / end must now wait. | And tell me,

Chorus:
when will our eyes meet? | When can I touch you? | When will this

strong yearn-in' end? | And when will I hold you a-

1.
gain?

2.
Bridge:
36
C F/C C/G F/G C/G
gain? I feel the change com - in', I feel the wind
mf
40
F/G C/G F/G Gm7 C7
blow, I feel brave and dar - ing, I feel my blood flow. With
45
F C/E Dm7 C F
you, I could bring out all the love that I have. With you, there's a
50
C/E D7 F/G G7
heav - en, so earth ain't so bad. And tell me,

Chorus:

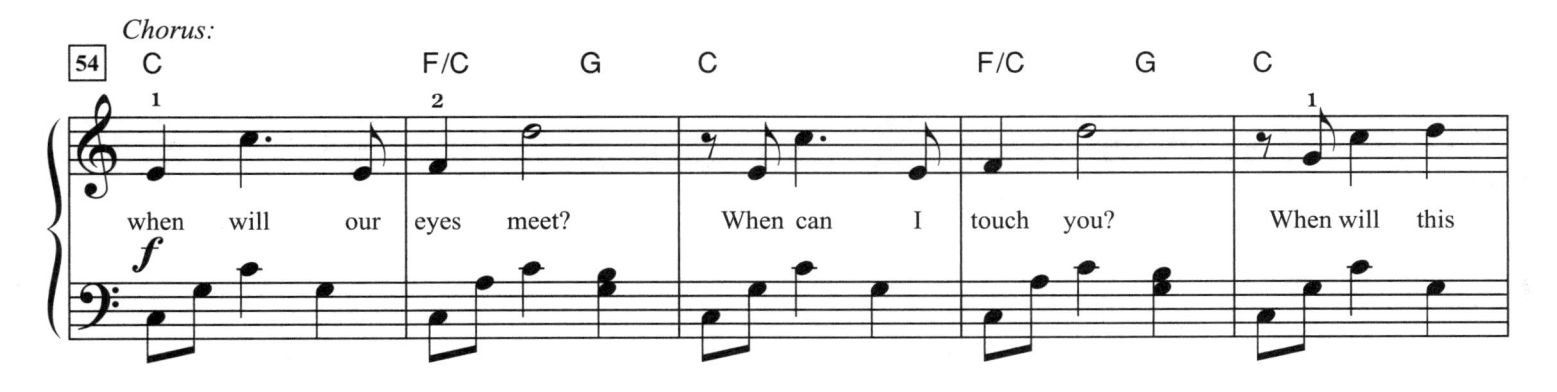

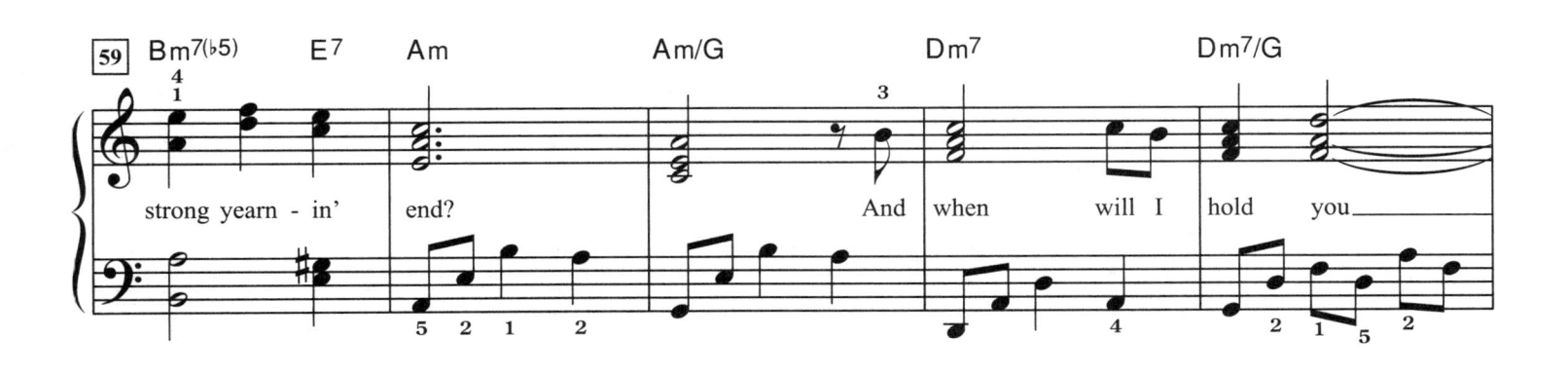

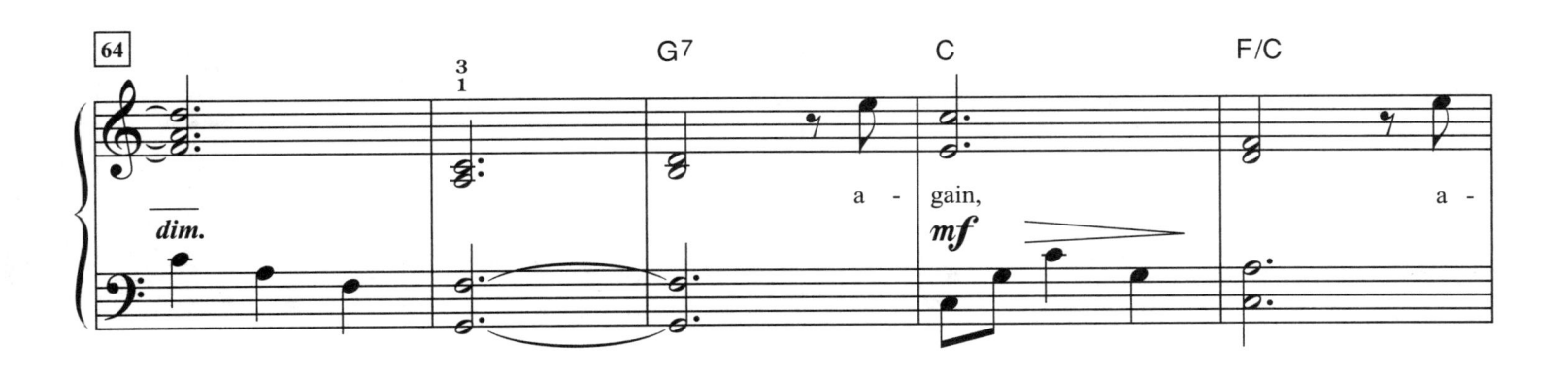

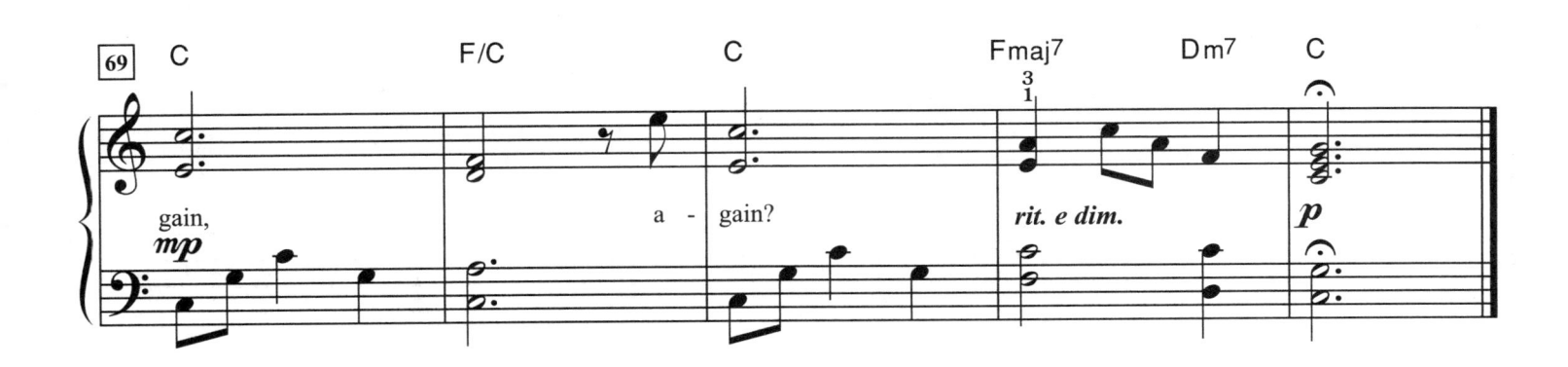

when will our eyes meet? When can I touch you? When will this strong yearn-in' end? And when will I hold you a-gain, a-gain, a-gain?

WHEN A MAN LOVES A WOMAN

Words and Music by
Calvin Lewis and Andrew Wright
Arranged by Dan Coates

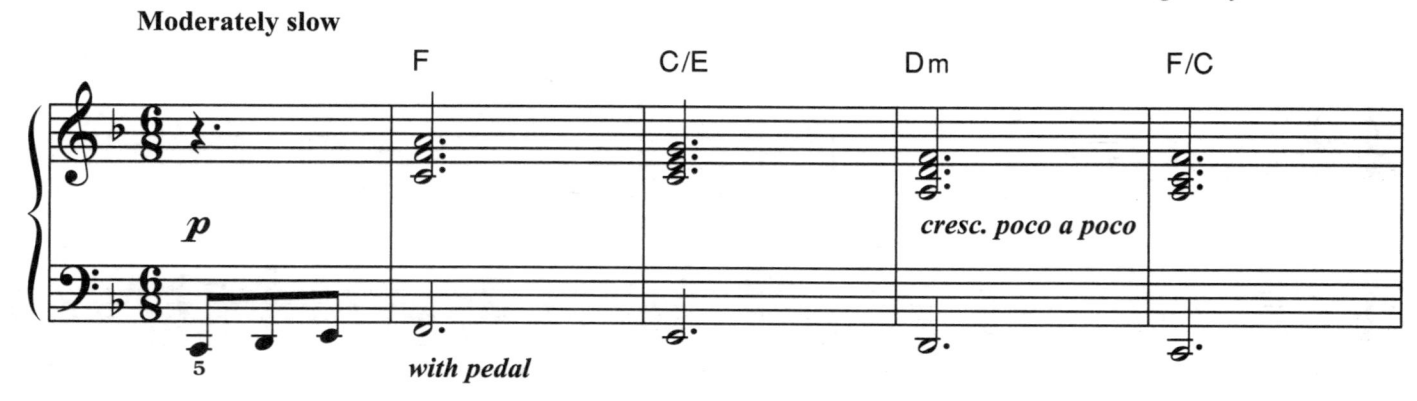

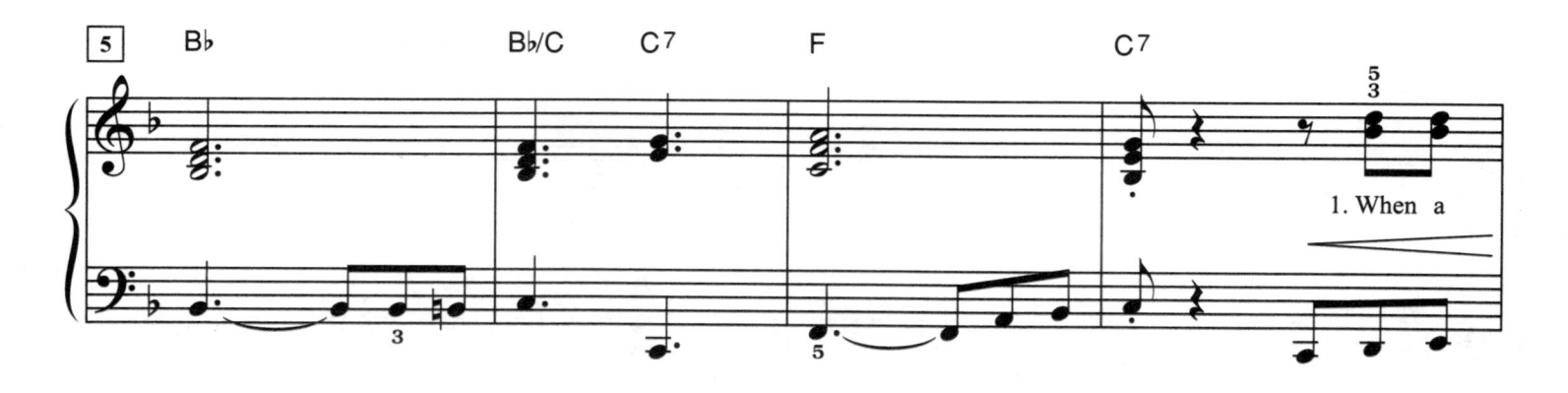

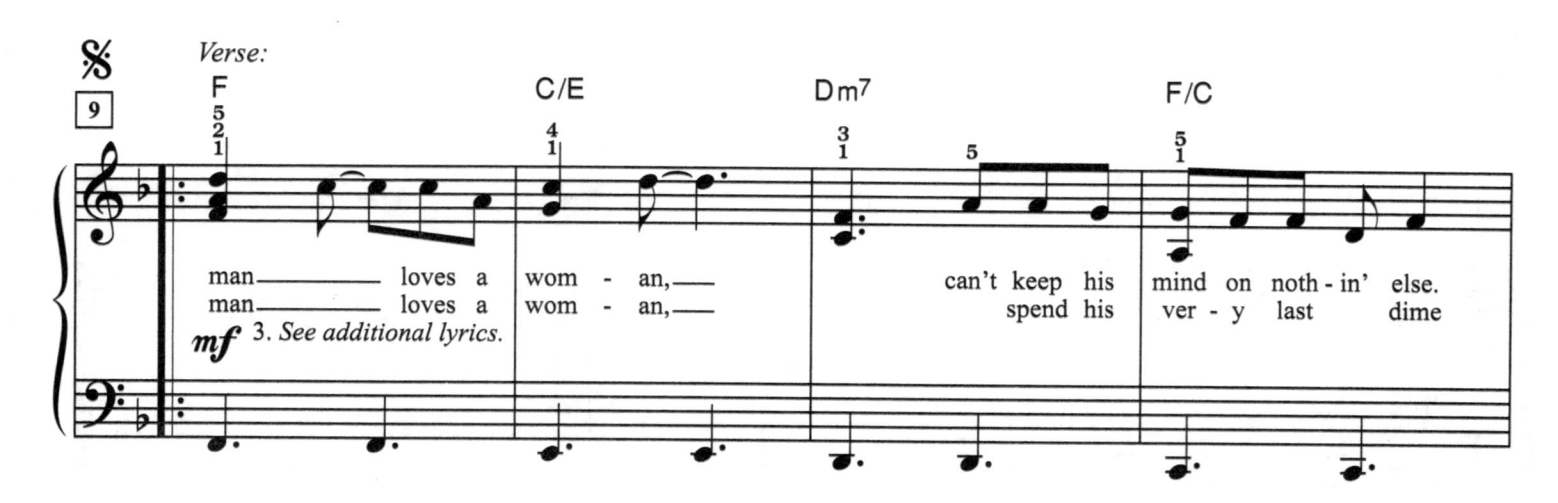

13
B♭ C B♭/C F B♭/C
He'd trade the world for the good thing he's found. If she is
try - ing to hold on to what he needs. He'd give up
17
F C/E Dm7 F/C
to Coda
bad, he can't see it. She can do no wrong.
all his com - forts and sleep out in the rain,
21
B♭ C7 F
1.
Turn his back on his best friend if he puts her down.
if she said that's the
24
B♭/C C7 F F7
2.
2. When a way it ought to be.
cresc.

Bridge:
28
B♭
F
F7
f
When a man loves a woman,
32
B♭
F
F7
I give you ev - 'ry - thing I've got.
36
B♭
F
C/E
Dm7
Try - ing to hold on to your pre - cious love.
40
G7
C7sus
C7
D.S. al Coda
Ba - by, ba - by, please don't treat me bad.
3. When a

Loving eyes can never see.

When a man loves a woman,

(Play 3 times)

When a man loves a woman.

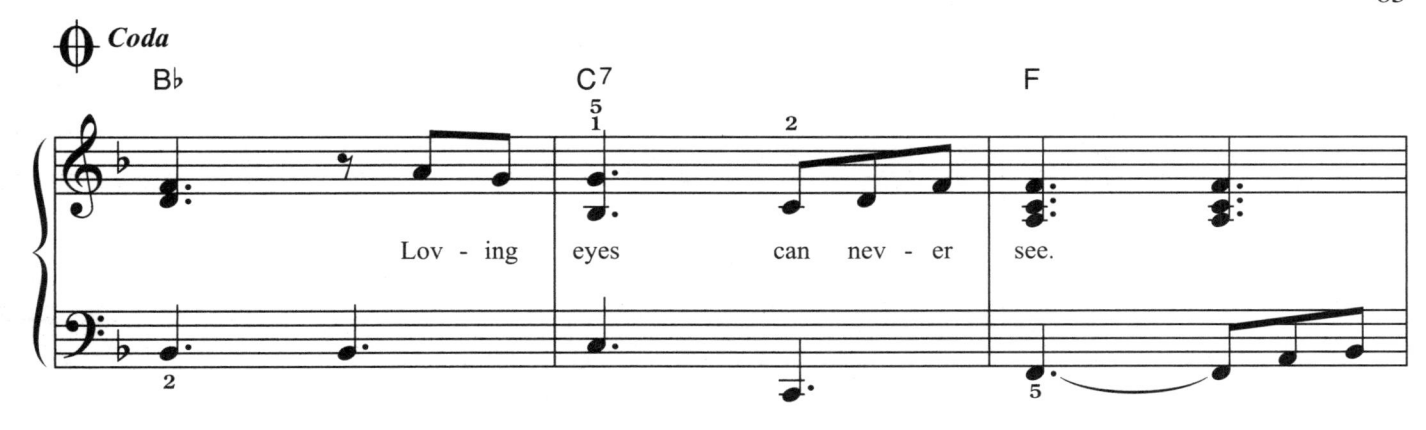

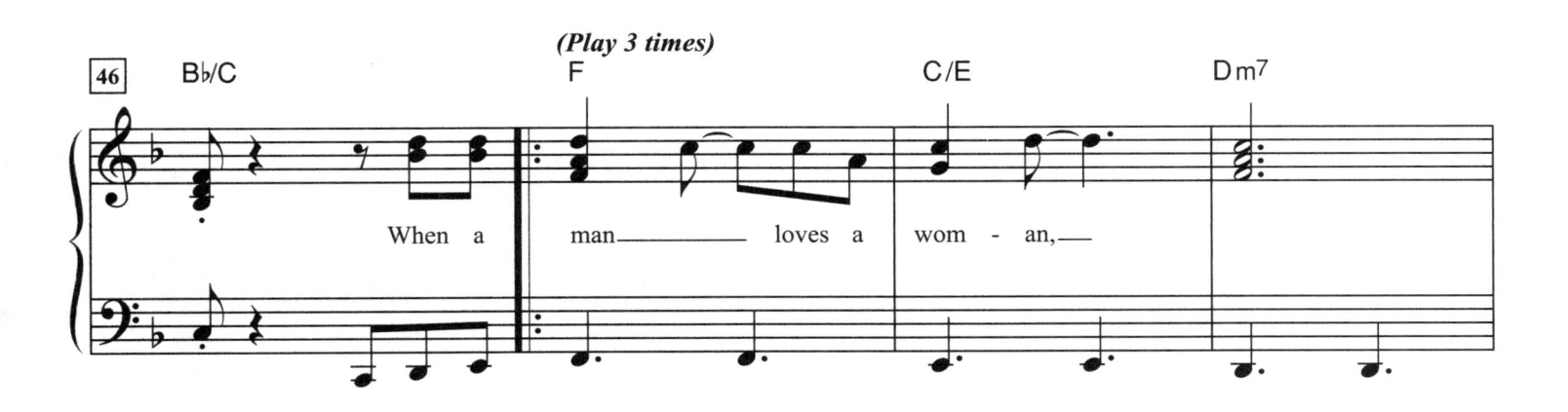

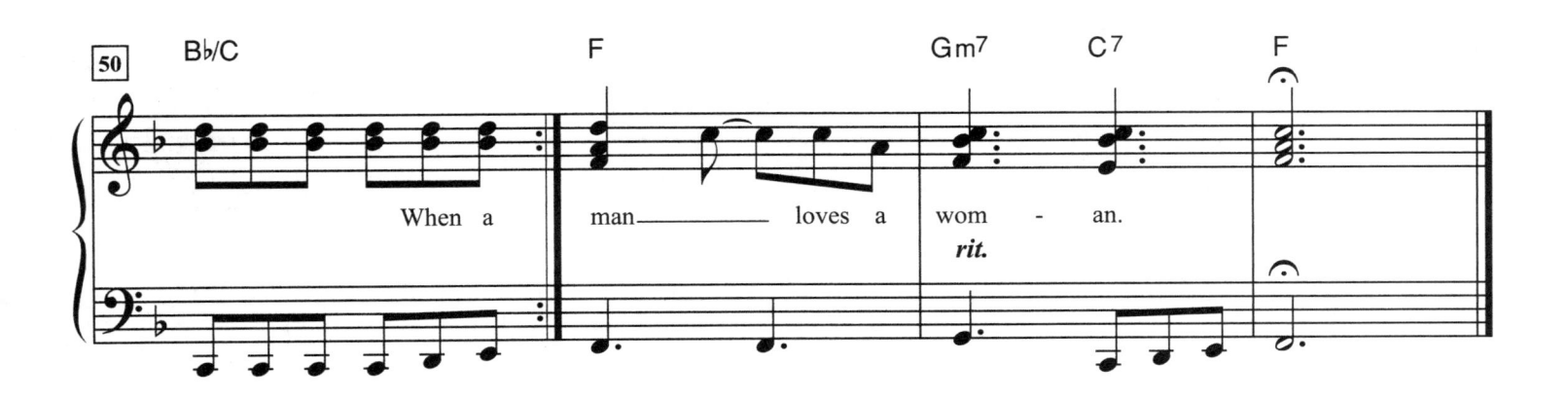

rit.

Verse 3:
When a man loves a woman,
Deep down in his soul,
She can bring him such misery.
If she is playing him for a fool,
He's the last one to know.
Loving eyes can never see.

WHEN YOU TELL ME THAT YOU LOVE ME

Words and Music by
Albert Hammond and John Bettis
Arranged by Dan Coates

Moderately slow

with pedal

Verse:
1. I wan-na call the stars down from the sky. I wan-na live a day that nev-er dies. I wan-na change the world on-ly for you. All the im-pos-si-ble I wan-na do. I wan-na

© 1991 JOHN BETTIS MUSIC and ALBERT HAMMOND MUSIC
All Rights for JOHN BETTIS MUSIC Administered by WB MUSIC CORP.
All Rights for ALBERT HAMMOND MUSIC Administered by
WINDSWEPT PACIFIC ENTERTAINMENT CO. d/b/a LONGITUDE MUSIC
All Rights Reserved

85

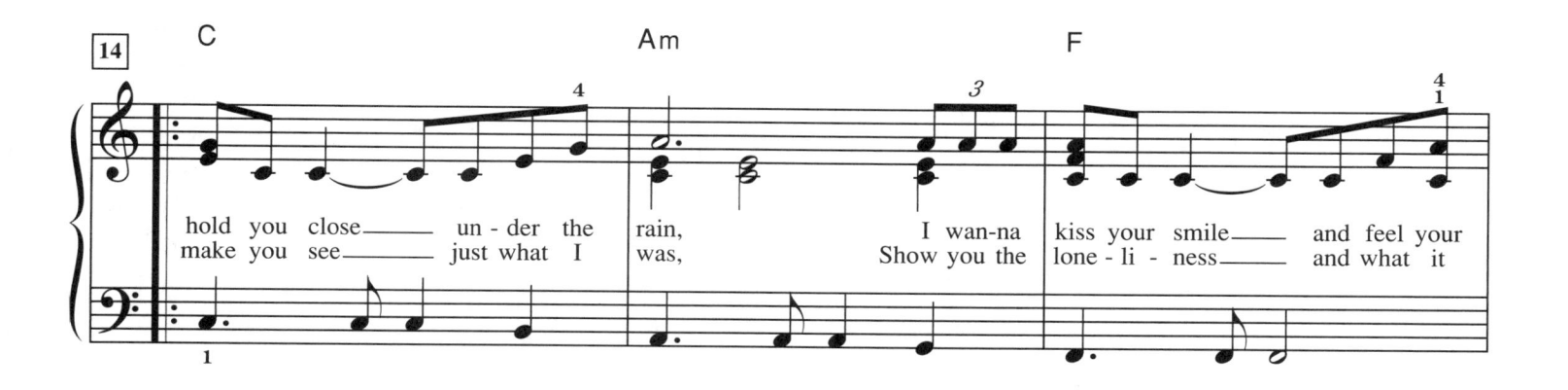

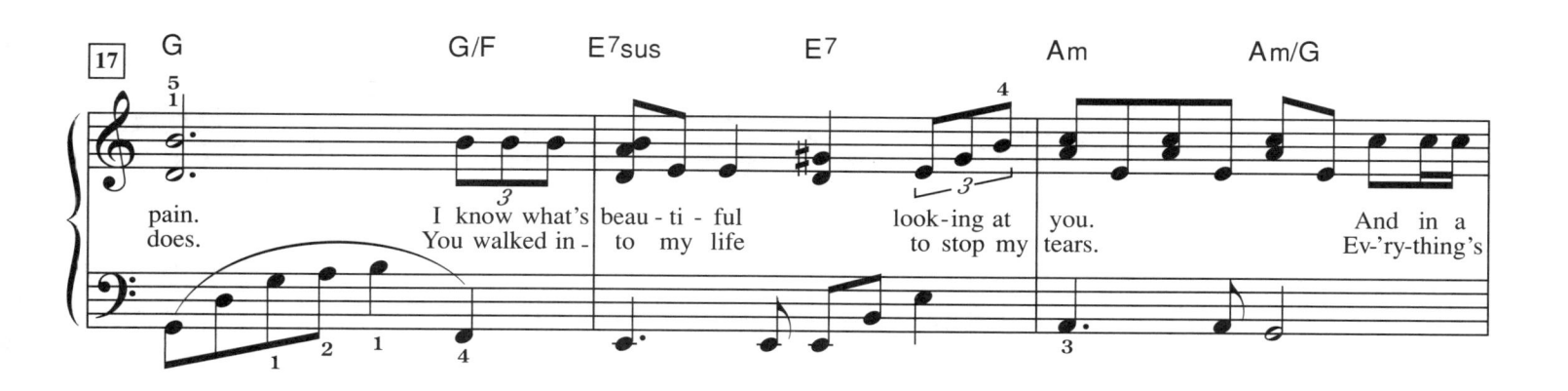

26
C
Am
F
Dm
an - y-thing you ask for,
nothing - ing is a-bove me. I'm
shin - ing like a can - dle in the
29
G7
1.
C
D/F♯
G7
dark
mf
when you tell me that you
love me.
2. I wan-na
mf
32
2.
C
Bridge:
A♭
C
love me.
mf
In a world with-out you,
I would al-ways hun-ger.
35
A♭
B♭7
A♭/B♭
B♭7
All I need is your love to
cresc.
make me strong - er.

Chorus:
37
E♭ Cm A♭ Fm
f Ev - 'ry - time you touch me, I be - come a he - ro. I'll make you safe no mat - ter where you
40
B♭7 A♭/B♭ B♭7 E♭ Cm
are. And bring you an - y - thing you ask for, noth - ing is a - bove me. I'm
43
A♭ Fm B♭7 E♭
shin - ing like a can - dle in the dark when you tell me that you love me,
46
Cm Cm7 A♭
when you tell me that you love me,
48
B♭7 E♭
when you tell me that you love me.
rit.